to David and Robyn

The KITE
that Won the
REVOLUTION

France to the Rescue!

1

JUNE 17, 1775. The American Revolution had begun. In Concord, Massachusetts, two months before, the American farmers had stood their ground and sent the British soldiers marching back to Boston under fire. But the British still held Boston, which was the heart and soul of the American cause. They had to be driven out.

On the night of June 16, then, American forces assembled on Breed's Hill in Charlestown, just across the river from Boston. They built fortifications on this hill and on nearby Bunker Hill and there they stood, a danger to every British soldier in Boston.

So on June 17, 1775, the British decided to drive the Americans from their barricades. At 2:30 P.M., British soldiers, gay and dashing in their red coats, marched up the hill in perfect order. From the Americans, crouched behind the breastworks, there was no sound.

"Don't fire until you see the whites of their eyes," the American commander, Colonel William

Prescott, had said. This was important, for the Americans had very little gunpowder. They could not afford to waste any of it. The British had to be close enough so that every American shot counted.

Up came the British, and, when they were almost upon the Americans, a volley of musket fire rang out. The British line was torn to shreds, and those who survived dashed down the hill again.

But the British were not easily beaten. The line was re-formed and back up they went, toward the place where the dead and wounded of the first attack lay. Again the Americans held their fire to the last minute and again the British line was torn and thrown back. If the battle had ended there, it would have been a terrific victory for the Americans, but it did not. A third time, the British line formed and moved upward, and now the Americans could do no more. They were out of ammunition.

Colonel Prescott gave the order to retreat and the Americans had to scramble out of their positions. It was the British turn to fire. A number of American soldiers, including the great patriot Joseph Warren, died under a volley of British bullets. The Americans could not answer the fire, for they had nothing more to shoot with.

Even so, it was a great day for the Americans. They had shown that they could stand up to the soldiers of the king. American hearts quickened as the

news of the Battle of Bunker Hill swept over the colonies.

But what if the American soldiers had had just a bit more ammunition? They might have driven the British out of Boston altogether. That was not to be. The British forces remained in the city all through the autumn and winter.

As spring of 1776 approached, there was talk of independence in many places. A Virginia planter, George Washington, was now commander in chief of the American forces.

And still the British were in Boston. In those days, though, the land on which Boston stood was almost an island. It was connected to the mainland by a narrow neck of land. Beyond that neck lay high ground called Dorchester Heights. In March of 1776, cannon came lumbering out of the west and George Washington lined them up on Dorchester Heights. From there, they could be used to bombard the British army in Boston and British ships in the harbor.

The British commander, William Howe, saw those cannon. He remembered Bunker Hill and decided to take no chances. On March 17, 1776, the British army sailed away from Boston, and no foreign army has ever walked the streets of that city again.

But where had the cannon come from? Did the Americans have cannon to fight with? Well, almost a year before, in May of 1775, a month before Bunker Hill, a young man named Ethan Allen had led a band of Vermonters westward. They called themselves the "Green Mountain Boys" and they were after Fort Ticonderoga, just across Lake Champlain. The British garrison at the fort was caught unprepared, and Ethan Allen's men captured them without trouble.

The Green Mountain Boys also captured the fort's cannon, and dragged them by ox team a hundred and fifty miles eastward to the little American army camped outside Boston. It was those British cannon that drove the British out of the city, for the Americans had no cannon of their own.

The Americans were not to have many triumphs in the next year or two. It was the same problem as at Bunker Hill — a continual shortage of supplies: no guns, no powder, sometimes no food.

If the colonists had only had supplies, things might have ended in their favor quickly. The British King, George III, was not popular at home and some of the British generals were not eager to fight the war. General William Howe in particular let the American troops escape several times when he might have crushed them.

The British people did not like the war either. So few of them volunteered to fight, that George III had to hire German soldiers from Hesse ("Hessians") to fill out his army. What's more, the British had to ship their men three thousand miles across the ocean, and in the 1700's such a voyage took months.

Still, the British navy controlled the seas and those soldiers arrived. What's more, they arrived with plenty of supplies. The British never ran out of gunpowder. Against the trained British soldiers were untrained American farm boys who signed up for a few months, then went home. George Washington could hardly keep even a tiny army together and he lost battle after battle.

In September 1776, General Howe, having given up Boston, captured New York instead. Washington's little band was forced into a heartbreaking retreat across New Jersey, but Washington himself did not lose courage. In Pennsylvania, he suddenly turned. On Christmas night in 1776, he moved quietly back across the Delaware River and, in a lightning stroke, captured nearly a thousand Hessians at Trenton.

That kept hope alive, but the British were still winning. Their General, John Burgoyne, marched southward from Canada toward Albany. Howe, who should have marched north to meet Burgoyne,

sailed for Philadelphia. In September 1777, Howe captured Philadelphia, and the two largest cities in the colonies, New York and Philadelphia, were in British hands.

To be sure, Burgoyne's army was slowly worn away and in October 1777, he was forced to surrender at Saratoga. This was a tremendous victory for the Americans. A British army had seldom surrendered on the field of battle, but this one did.

Yet even so, the British did not give up, and soon the Americans were worse off than ever. In the winter of 1777, while the British army was snug in Philadelphia, Washington's soldiers were freezing and starving to death at Valley Forge, twenty miles to the west. The American cause was at rock bottom.

How had the Americans lasted even this long? That they lasted at all was due to the fact that guns, ammunition, and other supplies, were being sneaked into the colonies from France. It wasn't enough; it was far from enough. However, it let the Americans hang on by their fingernails.

Then, on February 6, 1778, with Washington at Valley Forge and the American cause nearly dead, France entered into an open alliance with the Americans. Supplies came at a faster pace and the Revolutionary forces could take on new hope.

A French fleet crossed the ocean to help the struggling young nation. It fought off the British

just long enough to allow French soldiers to be brought to the American shores. At the siege of Yorktown, which ended the war, French troops served with Americans under Washington, and a French fleet stood out at sea. It is quite likely that without French help, the United States would never have won its independence.

Well, then, why did the French help?

One reason, of course, was that France was a traditional enemy of England. Ever since the Norman invasion of England in 1066, English and French armies had been fighting. For a while, during the 1400's, English armies under Henry V had almost conquered France.

In later centuries, they continued to fight, and the French usually lost. In the late 1600's and early 1700's, England had fought against the French King, Louis XIV, and had beaten him. In the middle 1700's, England had fought against the next French King, Louis XV, and had beaten him too. The war against Louis XV was called the Seven Years' War in Europe, but in North America it was called the French and Indian War.

As a result of the Seven Years' War, which ended in 1763, Great Britain had taken the colonies of Canada and India from France. Now under a new

King, Louis XVI, France was quite ready for revenge.

However, was it wise to interfere in this fight between Great Britain and her colonies? If France tried to take part, might she not be beaten again and be worse off than ever? The French Foreign Minister was Count Charles Gravier Vergennes. He was anxious to recover France's position in the world, but he was also a wise man, and he saw that there were difficulties.

For one thing, he didn't believe a handful of untrained colonists could stand up forever against the skilled British armies. There was no point in helping the colonists, if they were sure to be beaten, and France would then have to face an angry Britain.

Secondly, France was in terrible condition. The government had no money; it was practically bankrupt. How could France stand the expense of a war with Great Britain, even if things went well? The French people themselves were likely to become restless.

There was a third point, and the most important. The Americans were fighting for liberty, they said, and against British tyranny. However, the British government was far milder than the French monarchy. France was ruled by an extravagant aristocracy, and the French people had no liberty at all.

Should France be so foolish as to help a bunch of
Revolutionaries who went about saying, "All men
are created equal"? Should they help Americans
revolt against their king and set up a government
of the people? Would not the French people decide
they could do the same? Might they not revolt
against their king as well?

For two years, Count Vergennes thought of all
these dangers and did his best to keep France from
getting into the war. He was forced to send some
money and supplies secretly, but he did as little as
possible. And he was right to be cautious. In the
end, when he was forced into the war after all, the
result was disaster for the French monarchy even
though France won a victory.

The French government had more financial troubles than ever as a result of the war, and the French
people were worse off than ever. The French
watched the Americans building a new government of the people for themselves, and felt it was
their turn.

In 1789, six years after the end of the American
Revolution, the French people rose in rebellion.
Vergennes had died two years before that, but if he
had lived, he would have been able to say, "I told
you so."

Why then did Vergennes enter the war? What
forced him in? One of the reasons was that many of

the French aristocrats, who ran the country, were on the side of the Americans. One young French nobleman, the Marquis de Lafayette, only nineteen years old, sailed enthusiastically for America to serve without pay under Washington. Others kept putting pressure on Vergennes and on King Louis XVI. Help the Americans, they kept saying. Help the Americans.

This was foolish of them in a way. The aristocrats should have been the last people to want to see American notions of freedom and equality win out, for if the French people picked up those notions, it would be the end of the aristocrats.

And it was. The French Revolution, when it

came, was their death. Hundreds of the aristocrats died under the guillotine. Louis XVI was executed in 1793 and Queen Marie Antoinette in 1794.

Couldn't the French aristocrats have seen that it was dangerous for them to help revolutionaries anywhere in the world?

Well, they didn't. One reason they didn't was that they all fell into a head-over-heels fit of admiration for a particular American. On December 21, 1776, half a year after Bunker Hill, an American had arrived in France. He was an old man of nearly seventy-one. The top of his head was bald, and the white hair at the sides and back fell down in waves to his shoulders. He dressed plainly and carried a thick staff to help him walk. His eyes twinkled from behind round glasses. His name was Benjamin Franklin.

The French aristocrats, with their powder and wigs, their silk stockings, swords, and brocades, could never get enough of him. He charmed them all, and all they wanted to do was help the old man and his country.

It is quite likely, then, that if it were not for Benjamin Franklin, the French might not have helped the Americans, and the United States might not have won its independence. But why should the aristocrats have thought so highly of this plain

American? What had Franklin done to make himself the toast of France?

A quarter of a century earlier, in 1752, Benjamin Franklin had flown a kite while a thunderstorm gathered overhead. You may not think there is much to flying a kite, but when Franklin did so, he made himself world famous. He made himself one of the most admired and respected scientists in the world. He made himself the *only* American known by name to the cultivated men of Europe. You might say, then, that it was Franklin's kite that won the Revolution. It was Franklin's kite that allows us to live in an independent United States of America today.

In this book, I will try to explain how this came about. To do so, I shall have to go back in time, back to ancient Greece. In fact, I shall have to go back far beyond that, back to a time forty or fifty million years in the past.

In those days, there were no men on the earth, but, in what is now northern Europe, there grew large forests made up of trees something like the pine trees of today. Those forests are now long gone and no such trees grow any longer. It is, however, with those trees that the story starts.

Gold from the Sea

2

PINE TREES produce a gummy, sticky liquid when the bark is cut or damaged in any way. When this sticky liquid has stayed in contact with the air for a while, it hardens into a yellow-brown solid. This solid protects the spot where the bark was damaged.

Because this liquid flows out of cut portions of the pine tree, it came to be called *resin,* from a Greek word meaning "to flow."

The trees I mentioned at the end of the previous chapter produced resin in tremendous quantities. Some scientists think they must have developed a kind of disease that made them produce endless amounts of it. Perhaps it was this disease that killed them in the end. That may be why no more such pine trees, of this particular variety, exist.

The resin produced by the trees still exists, however. It lies buried under feet of soil. Most of it lies under a stretch of ocean that has come in to bury the place where the huge forest once stood. That bit of ocean, in the north of Europe, is now called the Baltic Sea.

When there is a storm, bits of the old resin are

washed up on the southern shores of the Baltic. There is even a place on the southern shores where the resin can be dug out of the ground, as though it were a mineral.

Many pieces of this ancient resin are of a clear and attractive reddish-yellow color. We call it *amber* and the same word is used to describe the color of the resin.

The color and appearance of amber have always been greatly admired. Because it is so admired, "Amber" can sometimes be used as a girl's name. The German word for it is *Bernstein,* and that is sometimes used as a last name among people whose native language is German.

Amber is much softer than ordinary minerals found in the ground. It is not a rocky mineral, after all, but only a kind of solidified tree sap. This means that it is easy to carve amber into pretty shapes. This was particularly important in very ancient times when there weren't the proper tools for handling hard materials.

Even before the dawn of history, the primitive people of Europe were trading pieces of this pretty stone that was so easy to carve. People near the Baltic Sea would exchange pieces of amber for something else that they wanted. Thus, amber slowly made its way southward.

The ancient Greeks, hundreds of miles away on

the Mediterranean Sea, acquired amber in this way. They admired it and made ornaments of it, and they called it *elektron* from a word that meant "gleaming" or "shining," because the amber, when polished, shone as yellow as the sun. (The Greeks gave the same name to gold, for the same reason. Indeed, amber is sometimes called "gold from the sea.")

The Romans changed the Greek word to *electrum*. They discovered where it came from. In the time of the Emperor Nero, an expedition to the shores of the Baltic returned with 6½ tons of amber. Nowadays, there have been times when those same shores produced over 500 tons of amber in a single year.

Amber is still used, even today, for costume jewelry, for cigarette-holders and pipe mouthpieces, and so on. Far more important is the fact that amber is useful to scientists.

In the old pine forests of millions of years ago, an insect may have landed on some oozing sap while it was still soft. More resin would surround and bury it even as it struggled to get away. The resin then hardened, with the insect inside.

Now pieces of amber are found which contain insects that are millions of years old but which are still perfectly preserved. Scientists have managed to study insects of types that are no longer alive.

Pine needles are preserved, as well as bits of wood and quantities of pollen. Amber is almost a window into the northern world of the pine forests of fifty million years ago.

But this is not all that amber has done for science. Amber has done much more, and it did it 2500 years ago on the shores of Asia Minor. In 600 B.C., the city of Miletus (my-lee'tus) stood on the eastern shores of the Aegean Sea. Those shores are now part of the nation of Turkey, but, in ancient times, Greek-speaking people lived there. Miletus was one of the most civilized and cultured of the cities that made up ancient Greece, and one of her citizens was a philosopher named Thales (thay'-leez).

Thales was a scientist; the first scientist in history whose name we know. He studied the heavens and the earth and tried to discover the rules that lay behind their workings.

When Thales heard tales of mysterious rocks that pulled iron toward themselves, he investigated at once. He found samples of what we now call *lodestone*. He had obtained this rock from a place near a town called Magnesia about thirty miles northeast of Miletus. He named the rock for the town and we still call objects that attract iron, *magnets*.

Thales studied magnets but he didn't quite know what to make of them. It was very strange that a

dead rock should pull iron to itself. It was so strange that Thales wondered if the rock were really dead. He felt that it might be alive in some ways and might have a soul such as human beings had.

Naturally, he tried other kinds of rocks to see if they might have souls also that would enable them to attract iron. He must have felt that if something as unattractive as black lodestone had a soul, surely pretty objects might have one. Yet gold did not attract iron, nor did silver. But what about amber? It was almost as attractive as gold and it had a similar color. No, it had no soul, either.

But one of the attractive things about amber is that it has a faint, pleasant odor. This odor can be made stronger by rubbing. Perhaps Thales sat rubbing a piece of amber as he thought about what magnetism might mean. Perhaps he put the amber down near a piece of fluff and noticed later that the fluff was sticking to the amber.

At any rate, he experimented and found that amber didn't attract anything ordinarily, but did begin to attract when it was rubbed — especially on a dry day. It would pick up light bits of thread or feathers.

Amber, too, had a soul, then; but it was a different kind of soul than lodestone had, a more amazing one. Lodestone attracted only iron, but rubbed amber attracted anything.

This was a very curious thing indeed and it must have made amber seem even more valuable. No doubt the ancients suspected there was some magical value to jewelry made out of it. Little human figurines, made out of amber, sold for high sums in the days of ancient Rome.

As the centuries passed, however, magnets proved more interesting than rubbed amber. For one thing, magnetic attraction was the stronger of the two. It was found that steel needles could be made into magnets if they were stroked with lodestone for a period of time. Such metal magnets were even stronger than lodestone.

Then, too, sometime in the Middle Ages, it was discovered that if a magnetized needle were placed on a cork which was allowed to float in water, the needle would always turn so it pointed north. The first European we know of who described this behavior of a magnetized needle was a Frenchman named Peter Peregrinus ("Peter the Pilgrim"). He wrote about it in 1269.

This was a very exciting thing to find out about a magnet. All through ancient times, men who traveled the sea had not dared move very far away from land. Far out on the ocean, with water all around, it would have been too easy to get lost.

On clear nights, to be sure, they could guide

themselves by the North Star, for that was always in the same place in the sky. But what if they hit a cloudy spell?

But here was a magnetic needle pointing out the north all the time, clouds or not. This gave sailors their directions and they would always be able to calculate the direction in which they had left land and, therefore, the direction in which they would find land again. With the needle as a guide, they couldn't be lost.

The needle was pinned on a card in such a way as to leave it free to pivot. The card was marked with a circle on which the different directions were indicated. The needle was "encompassed" (that is, surrounded) by these direction markings, so the instrument came to be called a *compass*.

Once the European mariners learned to use the compass, they began to strike out more and more boldly into the ocean. The Age of Exploration began and the world opened up. Columbus would not have dared make his voyage across the Atlantic if he did not have compasses on board ship. So you see, it was Thales's magic stone that led to the discovery of the New World.

But while the lodestone was doing so much for mankind, what of rubbed amber? Nothing at all, I'm afraid. It was not until the late 1500's that an

Englishman took up the study of amber where
Thales had left off twenty-two centuries before.

The Englishman was William Gilbert. He was a
physician by profession and a successful one, too.

Toward the end of his life he was physician to
Queen Elizabeth I. In his spare time, though, he
conducted scientific experiments.

His chief interest was magnetism and, in 1600,
he published a book in which he described his experiments. He explained why he had decided that
the whole earth was something like a huge magnetic needle with its ends in the direction of the
North Pole and the South Pole.

But ever since 1570, he had also been studying

the attracting powers of amber. He made himself a light metal arrow which he pivoted on a needle in such a way that it was perfectly balanced. If he rubbed amber and brought it near the metal arrow, the arrow turned to face the amber. The arrow moved so easily that Gilbert could detect very faint attractions, indeed.

Gilbert wondered if amber were the only object which would show attractive powers when it was rubbed. Now that he had a device to detect very faint attractions, perhaps he should try materials other than amber.

Since amber was a kind of semi-precious jewel, it was natural to try other jewels. To Gilbert's surprise, he found that a number of them behaved just as amber did. Among the stones that did so were diamond, sapphire, amethyst, opal, carbuncle, jet, and even ordinary rock crystal. On the other hand, a number of substances, including all the metals that Gilbert tried, did not attract anything, no matter how hard or how long they were rubbed.

What shall we call these substances? Some of them acted like amber when rubbed and some did not. We might speak of "amber-like substances" and "non-amber-like substances," if Gilbert had been writing in English. In his day, however, scholars wrote in Latin.

In Latin, the word for amber was *electrum*, as I

said. Consequently, Gilbert spoke of *vis electrica* when he meant "the force in amber." Because of this phrase, substances which acted like amber came to be called *electrics*. The others, of course, are *non-electrics*.

About 1650, the force of attraction produced by rubbed amber was given a new name by an English writer named Walter Charleton. It is now one of the most familiar scientific terms in existence. The word, which comes straight from the Greek and Roman names for amber, the gold from the sea, is, of course, *electricity*.

The Ball of Sulfur

3

GILBERT's work had come at a time when a new age was dawning.

In Italy, a scientist named Galileo was also experimenting. In particular, he studied the manner in which objects fell, and worked out simple mathematical ways of describing the movements. He wrote such interesting books about his experiments, that other scholars began to think it might be fun to experiment.

Some of them experimented with Gilbert's electrics, but not much is known about those experiments. Little by little, it was found that the harder and longer one rubbed an electric, the more electricity it came to contain.

To get a good amount of electricity meant that a lot of effort had to be put into rubbing, and sooner or later someone was bound to try some trick to make the rubbing easier.

The first to do so was a German, Otto von Guericke (gay'rih-kuh). He was mayor of the German town of Magdeburg from 1646 to 1681, but being mayor didn't stop him from experimenting.

In 1650, for instance, he became the first man ever to build an air pump. This was a device that could slowly pump the air out of a container, leaving a vacuum behind. One could do interesting things with a vacuum.

Thus, Guericke showed that a bell would not ring in a vessel from which the air had been pumped out. At least, it might ring, but the sound could not be heard. Sound would not travel through a vacuum.

Then, in 1654, he prepared two metal hemispheres that fit snugly together. One had a nozzle attached and through that nozzle he pumped out the air, after the hemispheres had been put together very tightly.

Using chains, Guericke attached a team of horses to a handle on one hemisphere and a second team to a handle on the other. He drove the teams of horses in opposite directions but the hemispheres held together. However, when Guericke let the air back into the hemispheres, they fell apart by their own weight.

Men were just beginning to understand about air pressure in those days. Watching those "Magdeburg hemispheres" stick together, with just thin air holding them shut, astonished everyone. The German Emperor himself, Ferdinand III, watched one of these demonstrations. Guericke found himself famous.

In the 1660's, Guericke turned to the problem of electricity. He discovered something new and interesting about amber. If he rubbed a piece of amber very hard and then pressed it between his fingers, he made it crackle. If he did the experiment in the dark, with every crackle, Guericke could see a tiny little flash of light. Sometimes, he managed to get quite a noticeable spark.

This was exciting, of course, but the constant rubbing and pressing must have gotten on Guericke's nerves. What he needed was some way to collect a large quantity of electricity without all this hard rubbing and rubbing. Perhaps a large piece of material was what he needed. Surely a large "electric" would hold more electricity than a small one.

But it was difficult to get a really large piece of amber or a large diamond, or a large amethyst. Something else was needed; something cheap and common that came in big pieces.

He thought of sulfur. Perhaps he thought of it because of the sparks he had pulled out of amber. Perhaps the eerie glow of sparking amber in the dark reminded him of the eerie glow of burning sulfur. Anyway, sulfur was easy enough to get and quite cheap. It was certainly worth trying.

Guericke therefore obtained a quantity of sulfur and melted it. He poured the melted sulfur into a

large, round glass flask, and stuck a wooden rod with a crank attachment into the hot liquid. Then he let the sulfur cool and become solid.

When he broke the glass, out came a large yellow ball of sulfur, larger than his head. He put it down into a wooden holder so arranged that he could turn the ball of sulfur by means of the crank, without much effort. He then put his hand on the turning sulfur.

As the sulfur was rubbed in this fashion, it gained electricity. The more he turned and rubbed, the more it gained. Much more electricity could be piled up in the large sulfur ball than in any small piece of amber.

In this way, Guericke constructed the first *electrical friction machine.*

He used it to make several important discoveries. He found that electricity didn't always attract. Sometimes, it pushed a light object away. Thus, there was *electrical repulsion* as well as *electrical attraction.*

Guericke also found that if some object were brought near his ball of sulfur, that object sometimes showed an attractive force. Electricity was induced in it just by the presence of electricity in the nearby ball of sulfur. This is *electrical induction.*

Guericke's work also helped make experimenting

fashionable. In ancient times, you see, the great Greek thinkers had usually felt that experimenting was a little beneath them. Experimenting meant working with one's hands, and physical labor was only for mechanics and slaves. The true philosopher, they felt, should spend his time thinking.

But now, in the 1600's, men like Gilbert, Galileo, and Guericke were showing the world what could be done by experimenting. Interesting things could be discovered that the ancients never dreamed of. Experimenting, therefore, was no longer for mechanics and slaves only. Well-bred gentlemen couldn't resist trying their hands at it.

In the middle 1600's, in England, a group of gentlemen met occasionally to talk about the new scientific discoveries. They were well-educated men, usually with some money of their own, and they had the spare time to experiment for themselves. They described these experiments and discussed the results among themselves.

In the 1660's, the British King, Charles II, grew interested in their work. He granted them a special charter and they began to call themselves the Royal Society of London for Improving Natural Knowledge. Usually, the organization is just called the Royal Society.

It was an exciting time. Great discoveries were

being made on every hand. New instruments revealed things that no one had ever seen before.

Back in 1608, a Dutch spectacle-maker had invented a tube with lenses at each end. Distant things viewed through such a tube seemed very close. Galileo improved the tube the next year and called it a *telescope*. He turned it on the heavens.

There he saw stars too faint to be seen without a telescope — thousands of them. He saw mountains on the moon and spots on the sun. He looked at the planet Jupiter and found it had four little moons circling it.

Lenses were also arranged to magnify very small objects. In Holland, a Dutch merchant, Anton van Leeuwenhoek (lay'ven-hook) took up the grinding of such lenses as a hobby. Through them he looked at tiny things and, in the 1660's, he discovered a new world of life. He found that ditch water was full of little "animalcules" too small to be seen without his *microscopes*.

The gentlemen of the Royal Society followed all such discoveries with great interest. In fact, Leeuwenhoek sent special reports on his discoveries to the Royal Society and they elected him a member.

An English gentleman and member of the nobility, Robert Boyle, was one of the founders of the Royal Society. He was a particular admirer of Galileo and Guericke.

Boyle built an improved vacuum-pump and he carefully studied the behavior of air when it was put under pressure. This was the first important work that led the way toward what we might call modern chemistry. It took the first step to the discovery of the steam engine and to the discovery of atoms.

But the greatest scientist of the 1600's, perhaps the greatest of all times, was another Englishman named Isaac Newton. In the 1660's, he found that white sunlight, if passed through a triangular block of glass (a "prism"), broke up into the different colors of the rainbow. These colors could be passed through another prism and recombined into white light.

He was only a young man in his twenties at the time, and this discovery made him famous. He became a professor at the University of Cambridge and went on to greater triumphs. He made important discoveries in mathematics. He built a new kind of telescope that was better in some ways than the kind that Galileo had used.

Most of all, he considered the experiments of Galileo with falling bodies and from that, he worked out the Three Laws of Motion. Newton used these laws of motion to study the motion of the moon around the earth. Eventually, he was able to show that the moon was falling toward the earth, just as an apple might be falling off a tree.

Although the moon was falling toward the earth, it never reached the earth, because it was also moving sideways to the earth. The combination of the two motions, down and sideways, kept the moon going round and round the earth.

Newton showed that, to describe the manner in which the moon fell toward the earth, one had to suppose that there was an attracting force of *gravity* between the moon and the earth. In fact, there was an attracting force of gravity between any two bodies, between the earth and the sun, for instance. That was what kept the earth going around the sun.

The other planets, too, were in the grip of the sun's attracting force.

This is called the Law of Universal Gravitation. Newton worked out a simple mathematical formula that showed just how the force of gravity changed with the size of objects and with the distance between them.

Newton's mathematical expression could be used to explain a great many things about the behavior of the heavenly bodies, and about the earth, too. It explained the existence of the tides, for instance, and why the earth was not a perfect sphere, but bulged at the equator.

Newton's work on the laws of motion and on gravity appeared in a great book, in the year 1683. It made a terrific impression on the scholars and learned men of Europe. They admired the way Newton had begun with a few simple assumptions and then, little by little, using a very clear line of mathematics, had developed his ideas and ended by explaining the behavior of the whole universe.

Suddenly, it seemed to European scholars that nothing could be hidden from this new way of experimenting. Surely, all problems could be solved if only one experimented like Galileo, then reasoned from the experiments like Newton.

Men felt so sure of this, and so confident that soon all problems would be solved by reason, that

the period from 1683 to 1789 is called the Age of Reason.

The study of the universe and of the behavior of objects in the skies and on earth had never been so popular as it was during the Age of Reason. And those who experimented had never been so respected.

One thing which completely interested the new experimenters was the strange force of electricity. By 1700, you see, there were three mysterious attracting forces known. The first to be discovered had been magnetism, and that had produced the compass. Through that the whole earth had been explored. The last to be discovered had been gravitation and Newton had used that to explain the universe.

But what about the third force, electricity? Surely great things would come out of that, too. Nothing had come out of it yet, but perhaps if someone experimented with electricity very carefully, he might make as great a name for himself as Newton did.

The scientists of the Age of Reason tackled electricity, therefore, with all their might.

The Two Fluids

4

FROM THE BEGINNING, scientists might well have wondered what electricity was. Thales' original idea had been that there was a kind of life in magnets and electrics.

This didn't satisfy the new scientists. Gilbert had rather sneered at people who believed such nonsense. But if electricity wasn't a form of life, what was it?

The first glimpse of a possible answer came through the work of an Englishman, named Stephen Gray. He was born in 1696, as the Age of Reason was starting, but certainly he wasn't a good example of the kind of experimenter one would expect to find in that time.

He was not in the least well-to-do and was probably not very well-educated. He didn't know about Guericke's work, for instance, and so he had to start from the beginning.

However, he did experiment skillfully and that really is all that counts. It is nice to be learned and well-to-do, but men without much silver in their

pockets, or learning in their heads, have done important work, too.

Like Guericke, Gray wanted a large object to electrify. In 1729, he began to use a long glass tube, about $3\frac{1}{2}$ feet from end to end, for the purpose. When he rubbed this, he found it could attract small feathers quite well, for glass was an electric. (Had Guericke known this, he might not have bothered melting sulfur in a large round glass flask. He might have used the flask itself.)

Gray's tube was open at both ends and this bothered him. He was afraid dust might get in and spoil his experiment. (Actually, the dust wouldn't have spoiled anything, but Gray didn't know that.)

To keep out the dust, he put corks into the openings at each end, and it's just as well he did, for that led to an important discovery. Gray found that when he rubbed the glass, little feathers were attracted to the corks as well as to the glass itself.

It was as though the electricity, whatever it was, had traveled from the glass into the corks. (Guericke had noticed that electricity seemed to travel from his sulfur ball through a length of thread, but he mentioned that very briefly in his writings. Besides, Gray had never read those writings and knew nothing about them.)

Gray proceeded, with great excitement, to try further experiments. He took a stick about four

inches long and put it into one of the corks. At the other end of the stick he placed an ivory ball. Next, he rubbed the glass. The glass attracted feathers, and so did the ivory ball, four inches away from the glass, even though he had not touched the ivory ball at all.

Gray tried sticking other things into the cork, longer pieces of wood, long metal rods. There was no mistake. The electricity traveled.

Until Gray's time, it had been assumed that when an object like amber, or any other electric, was rubbed, the electricity, whatever it was, stayed in the material and didn't budge. It was *static electricity* ("static" coming from a Latin expression meaning "to stand in place").

Gray's work, however, made it seem that the electrical force could move or flow from one object to another. Anything which flows is a *fluid* (a word which comes from a Latin term meaning "to flow"). Among the common objects about us, solids, such as wood and rock, cannot flow and are not fluids. Liquids such as water and oil, however, can flow, and are fluids. Air and other gases can also flow, so that they, too, are fluids.

This gives us two kinds of fluids: liquids and gases. Gases are "thinner" than liquids and have less "body." You can touch a liquid and feel it, but you can't seem to feel the air about you.

Perhaps, then, there is a third kind of fluid, the *electrical fluid,* which is even "thinner" and has less "body" than gases. It has so little "body" that it can flow through solid objects, though ordinary fluids cannot.

To be sure, no one could see the electrical fluid, but then no one could see air, either. You could be sure that air existed from its effects — from the action of wind, for instance. Well, you could be sure that electrical fluid existed from its effects.

Gray continued his experiments, trying to find out over how large a distance he could transmit the electrical fluid. He suspended his ivory ball from his glass electric by lengths of coarse twine up to thirty feet, and still found the ivory attracted feathers. (If the twine had been quite dry it would not have transmitted the fluid. Fortunately, in England's damp climate, the twine was not really dry.)

Gray wanted to try still longer stretches of twine, so he decided to pass it back and forth along his room, hanging it from nails in the ceiling. When he did this, however, he found that all at once the electrical fluid wouldn't pass through the twine at all. At least, no matter how he rubbed his glass tube, the ivory ball did not attract feathers.

What was wrong? What had spoiled the experiment?

The only thing Gray could think of were the nails. Before, the twine he used had not touched anything, but now it touched the nails. Could it be that the electrical fluid was passing through the twine, into the nails, and out through the ceiling, so that it never reached the ivory ball at all?

Suppose he tried something else. The nails were pretty thick and Gray decided to use something thin. The fluid might find it more difficult to pass through a thin object than through a thick one. Gray had some silk thread handy, so he suspended the twine by silk thread rather than by iron nails.

Now the experiment worked very well. The electrical fluid went through great lengths of twine, hundreds of feet of it, because it could not escape through the thin silk thread.

Very happily, Gray continued making this twine longer and longer, passing it back and forth across the room, until it grew so heavy that the silk threads broke.

Oh well, he'd just use something else that was very thin, but was stronger than silk. He got hold of thin brass wire, hung up his twine again, and suddenly, the electrical fluid was gone again.

Gray was astonished. It wasn't the thinness of the silk thread that kept the electrical fluid from passing through after all, because the fluid passed

through brass wire that was just as thin. It seemed that the electrical fluid didn't pass through the silk threads, because it couldn't pass through silk. It didn't matter whether the silk thread was thin or thick; the fluid wouldn't pass through. But the fluid could pass through iron or brass, whether the iron or brass were thin wires or thick nails.

In other words, Gray had found there were two kinds of substances: one through which the electrical fluid could pass, and one through which it could not pass.

Gray began to check a number of substances to see if the fluid would pass through them. He found it would not pass through amber, glass, horsehair, or sulfur. In fact, it would not pass through just those substances that could be electrified by rubbing. The fluid would pass through metals, however, and through other materials that could not be electrified by rubbing.

Gray thought about that. Perhaps the reason why some substances were electrics and some were not was because of the way they carried the fluid. A substance like amber or glass did not allow the fluid to pass through itself, so if any fluid were produced in them by rubbing, it stayed where it was. A substance like iron or brass did allow the fluid to pass. If any fluid were produced in iron or brass by

rubbing, it left quickly, and passed into anything else in the neighborhood.

If that were so, then suppose a piece of metal were surrounded by substances through which the fluid could not pass. Then the electrical fluid would not be able to leave the metal after all. What would happen?

In 1731, Gray placed pieces of metal on blocks of resin. When the metals were carefully rubbed with silk, electrical fluid appeared and had to stay. The metal then attracted light objects.

For one hundred fifty years, ever since Gilbert's time, scientists had thought metals were non-electrics, and now, Gray showed they could be electrics after all. In fact, everything could be an electric. Gray even suspended a young boy from the ceiling by silk wires and electrified him. A human being was an electric, too.

But if everything is an electric, there is no use in trying to divide objects into electrics and non-electrics, as Gilbert did. Instead, one should classify them as "substances that pass the electrical fluid and therefore seem non-electric," and "substances that don't pass the electrical fluid and therefore seem electric."

We have names for these two types of substances now. The names were not invented by Stephen Gray, but by another Englishman, just a few years

later, in 1736. This Englishman was John The-
ophilus Desaguliers (day-zah-goo-lyay') and his
name sounds so French because he was born in
France. His family came to England, however,
when he was only two years old.

Desaguliers suggested that substances through
which the electrical fluid passes, such as iron or
brass, be called *conductors*. After all, by making
such metals into wires, you can conduct the fluid
wherever you wish through them. Substances that
do not conduct the fluid, such as silk, are, of course,
non-conductors. For the non-conductors, Desaguliers suggested the name *insulators* (from a Latin
word for "island").

The word "insulator" is a good one. A conductor
can be made to keep its fluid if it is separated from
the rest of the world by non-conductors. The non-
conductors surround the conductor and make an
island out of it, so to speak.

Most of the work that had been done on electricity, from Gilbert's time on (except for Guericke's
experiments), had been done in England. But now
Frenchmen grew interested, too.

One of these was Charles François Du Fay, who
was superintendant of gardens for the king of
France. He repeated some of Gray's experiments
and improved on them. For instance, he found that

damp twine is an electrical conductor, while dry twine is an insulator.

But Du Fay's most important experiments were those which compared the electrical fluid in one substance with the electrical fluid in another. Ever since Gilbert had pointed out that there were numerous electrics, it had been taken for granted that the electricity in all of them was the same. But was that so?

In 1733, Du Fay rubbed a glass rod with silk, and filled the glass with electrical fluid so that it would attract light objects. He took two small pieces of cork and coated them with gold leaf. Then he hung them near each other by silk threads. He touched each piece of cork with the electrified glass rod. Naturally, some of the electrical fluid passed from the glass into the cork balls.

What happened then? Why, the two little cork balls did not attract each other at all. They repelled each other; they pushed each other away. Instead of hanging straight down, they hung away from each other. This was the electrical repulsion that Guericke had noticed half a century before, but Du Fay's experiment made the whole thing very clear and plain.

Apparently, then, when two objects were both filled with electrical fluid, they repelled each other. An electrified object only attracted something

which had no fluid in it. At least, so Du Fay decided.

Du Fay thought he could show this when he brought an electrified glass rod near a hanging cork ball that had not been electrified. It moved toward the glass rod at once, being attracted to it. As soon as it touched, however, it gained some of the fluid and it immediately moved away; it was now repelled.

So far, so good, but Du Fay wasn't finished. Would all electrics behave the same? If a long piece of resin is rubbed with wool, the resin is electrified. Sure enough, it then behaved just like the electrified glass. It attracted a cork ball that was not electrified, then, after the ball touched the resin and picked up the fluid, there was repulsion. And if two cork balls were each touched with the electrified resin rod, they repelled each other.

So far, Du Fay's theory was working perfectly, but he still wasn't finished. What if he touched a cork ball with an electrified glass rod, so that the cork ball gained fluid and was repelled by the glass rod? What if he next brought an electrified resin rod near the cork ball? Would it be repelled by the resin rod also?

Du Fay thought it would have to be, since the resin rod was also filled with fluid. However, to his surprise, the cork ball was not repelled by the resin rod. It was attracted by it, even though it was repelled by the electrified glass rod.

Du Fay then reversed matters. He touched an unelectrified cork ball with an electrified resin rod. Right away, the cork ball was repelled by the resin rod. But once that happened, it was attracted by an electrified glass rod.

Whatever an electrified glass rod attracted, an electrified resin rod repelled. And whatever an

electrified glass rod repelled, an electrified resin rod attracted.

When Du Fay tried other electrics, he found that they always fell into one class or the other. They either attracted and repelled whatever the electrified glass rod attracted and repelled, or they attracted and repelled whatever the resin rod attracted and repelled.

Du Fay, therefore, came to the decision that there must be two different types of electrical fluid. Either kind of fluid attracted objects that were not electrified, so that both glass rods and resin rods picked up lint and feathers.

However, if two objects both contained electrical fluid, then they attracted each other if each contained a different electrical fluid, but repelled each other if each contained the same electrical fluid.

Du Fay named the kind of electrical fluid in glass, *vitreous electricity* ("vitreous" comes from a Latin word for glass.) He named the other kind, the one in resin, *resinous electricity*.

Well then, if two cork balls are both filled with vitreous electricity, by being touched with an electrified glass rod, they repel each other. If both are filled with resinous electricity, by being touched with an electrified resin rod, they repel each other also.

If, however, one cork ball is touched by an elec-

trified glass rod, and the other by an electrified resin rod, the two balls contain different electrical fluids and attract each other.

This was an exciting new development, and meanwhile, other exciting things were happening, too. New electrical friction machines were being in vented.

The Shocking Jar

5

As I SAID in Chapter 3, Guericke had invented the first electrical friction machine, using sulfur. He didn't try anything else. Forty years later, an English experimenter, Francis Hauksbee, went about matters in more detail.

He rubbed a number of different kinds of substances, in order to find something more convenient than sulfur, and decided on glass. About 1706, then, he set up a glass globe which he could turn by a crank, just as Guericke's sulfur globe had been turned. The glass globe, however, did a better job of collecting electrical fluid when one's hand rubbed against it as it turned. Hauksbee got much better sparks out of his glass friction machine than ever Guericke got out of his sulfur.

Pretty soon, the glass globe was replaced by a glass cylinder, which was easier to handle. (Probably it was this cylinder which gave Gray the idea of using a long glass tube for his experiments.)

Other improvements were made, too. For instance, why use your hand to rub against the turning glass cylinder? It isn't a comfortable feeling and

one gets tired of standing there, anyway. A German professor, Johann Heinrich Winkler (veenk'-ler), invented a leather pad which was held against the glass by a spring. That was as good as a hand, and far less troublesome.

Once Gray had shown how conductors and non-conductors behaved, it was possible to move the electrical fluid from the friction machine and place it elsewhere.

For instance, you might hang a metal chain from one side of the turning glass cylinder. As the cylinder turned, the leather pad on one side filled it with electrical fluid through friction. The fluid passed from the cylinder into the chain on the other side. The lower end of the metal chain touched a metal plate so the electrical fluid passed into that. The metal plate was standing on an insulator, so that once the fluid entered the plate it could not leave. As the cylinder kept turning and rubbing against the leather pad, more and more electrical fluid was formed and passed into the plate.

You might imagine the plate as a kind of wagon into which you poured the electrical fluid till it was heaped up high. It was with this thought in mind, perhaps, that the plate came to be spoken of as highly *charged* when it was full of electrical fluid. "Charge," you see, comes from a Latin word mean-

ing "wagon." (The similar words, "car," "cart," "carriage," and "chariot," all come from that same Latin word.)

What happens, now, if that highly charged plate is allowed to come near something into which the electrical fluid can escape? After all, the plate is a conductor and the fluid within it can move about freely. If it can get out, it will do so at once.

One way of enabling it to get out is to *ground* it — that is, allow it to touch the ground. The ground is a pretty good conductor and will carry off the charge. It can be grounded if a man puts his hand near the plate, for a man's body is a pretty good conductor, too, and the fluid will pass through it and into the ground.

Ordinarily, the air, especially when it is dry, is a pretty good insulator. That is why the charge on the plate cannot escape if the plate is standing on an insulator. The electrical fluid cannot pass through the insulator into the ground. Neither can it pass into the air.

However, the amount of insulation the air offers depends upon its thickness. A thick layer of air is a far better insulator than a thin layer.

Suppose, then, you approach the charged plate with your finger. The electrical fluid in the plate cannot get into your finger because the air between is an insulator and will not conduct it. As your fin-

ger comes closer and closer, however, the width of air between finger and plate grows less and less. The air becomes a poorer insulator. Eventually, the width of air is so little that it will not insulate at all. The electrical fluid pours out of the plate, through the air, and into your hand.

The passage of the fluid makes the air glow, so that there is a spark. The spark heats the air, which expands and moves apart. The air contracts and comes together again as it cools. This movement of the air makes a sound, so that along with the spark there is a crackle.

The more heavily the plate is charged the brighter and longer the spark that is produced, and the louder the crackle.

All this, as you can see, is very much like magic to anyone who has never seen it. Suddenly, an ordinary piece of metal can produce sparks and crackles. What's more, when the spark enters the skin, it produces a tingly sensation that seems exciting and mysterious.

In the early 1700's, many people traveled about giving lectures on the new science of electricity, and they used friction machines for demonstrations. During the Age of Reason, the upper classes loved to attend such demonstrations, so they were usually very successful.

A particularly successful electrical friction ma-

chine was invented in 1745. Moreover, it was invented in two different places, and by two different men, at just about the same time.

It all came about because some experimenters noted that when a glass rod was charged, it didn't really keep its charge perfectly. Slowly, the charge got less and less, till it was gone altogether.

Nowadays, we know that there are substances in the air that do conduct electricity. These substances (present in only small quantities) carry off the charge, little by little. However, this was not known in the 1740's and, instead, some men reasoned it out as follows: If electricity is a kind of fluid, then it ought to act in many ways as other fluids do. It ought to act like water in some ways, for instance. Well, if drops of water were placed on a glass plate, they would slowly evaporate and disappear. Why shouldn't electrical fluid slowly evaporate and disappear too?

In order to eliminate the evaporation of water, it is placed in a closed vessel. Water in a closed vessel would remain there for years and years without evaporating. In that case, if electrical fluid were placed in a closed vessel, wouldn't that stay on for years without evaporating?

In 1745, a church official in eastern Germany, named E. G. von Kleist, thought he would try this. (Everyone was experimenting with electricity those

days, even church officials.) He therefore began with a bottle and cork. Of course he wanted something in the bottle which he could electrify, and one logical thing was water.

What he wanted to do, though, was to electrify the water without opening the bottle and letting the electrical fluid escape. For that reason, Kleist drove a long nail through the cork and into the

water. Now, if he used a friction machine and touched the nail to it, the electrical fluid would pass through the metal of the nail (which was a conductor, of course) and into the water.

Kleist did this. Once it was done, he thought he would check the little device and see if he had really electrified the water. He held the jar in one hand and put a finger to the nail sticking out above the cork. If the water were electrified, he would get a spark.

So he did, but what a spark! He felt as though a club had been brought down upon his arm. Nothing like this had ever been felt before. It was a real *electric shock*. That was enough for Kleist. He played with the device no more.

Almost immediately afterward, the same device was built by a Dutch professor. His name was Peter van Musschenbroek (mew'sen-brook) and he taught at the University of Leyden in the Netherlands.

Musschenbroek tested his little jar of water in the same way Kleist had, and with the same result. He got an electric shock that nearly knocked him unconscious and put him to bed for two days. "I would not take such a shock again," he wrote in a letter, "to become the King of France."

Unlike Kleist, however, Musschenbroek kept on experimenting (being very careful not to test the

bottle by hand). As a result, such bottles, or jars, came to be known as *Leyden jars,* from the name of the university.

Musschenbroek found pretty quickly that a spark could not be drawn off the metal above the cork, unless the jar were held in the hand, or unless the outside were touched by some conductor. Therefore, he began to coat the outside and the inside of the jar with a thin metal foil and that improved its performance. The sparks were better than ever.

To the early experimenters, it seemed that the electrical fluid in the Leyden jar must be pressed together or "condensed" so that a great deal of it fitted into the jar. That was why it gave off such bright sparks and strong shocks. For that reason, an instrument like the Leyden jar is called a *condenser* even today.

Then, too, the Leyden jar seemed to have a greater capacity to hold electrical fluid than ordinary objects. For that reason, such devices are also called *electric capacitors.*

You can well imagine that if lecturers were doing amazing things with friction machines before, they began to perform wonders after the Leyden jar was invented. They passed electrical fluid through thin wires in such quantities that the wire heated up and melted. They passed the fluid along as much as $2\frac{1}{2}$

miles of wet thread, and they passed it across lakes. They used electric shocks to kill small animals and birds.

Some particularly fancy tricks were tried by a French churchman, Abbé Jean Antoine Nollet (noh-lay'). He shocked himself with a Leyden jar, then decided that if the shock could be passed through a number of men, it would be spread out and weakened so that it wouldn't be so dangerous. It would also make a wonderful demonstration.

With King Louis XV, himself, watching, Nollet had 180 soldiers hold hands in a large circle. At one point, and only one, two soldiers were not holding hands. Nollet gave one of these soldiers a charged Leyden jar to hold and had the other soldier touch the metal knob. Out sprang the electric fluid and, quick as a flash, it passed through every one of the soldiers. Each felt the shock at the same time.

Later, Nollet did even better. He had 900 Carthusian monks line up in a circle that was a mile around, while members of the French aristocracy watched. This time several Leyden jars were used and, when the final one was touched and the circle completed, every single monk jumped up into the air at the same time — like super-trained dancers.

There must have been considerable applause.

But something far more important than Nollet's

tricks was happening, and in a place where scarcely
any scholar of the 1700's would have dreamed of
looking. It happened across the ocean in America.
So far, all through the 1600's and 1700's, the
amazing advance of the new science had been taking
place in just a few countries of western Europe.
Galileo had been an Italian, Gilbert an Englishman,
Guericke a German, Leeuwenhoek a Dutchman,
Du Fay a Frenchman. Cultivated Europeans would
never have dreamed that a real scientist could come
out of a place like the half-civilized American colonies. If they thought about America at all, it was
only as a place filled with barbarous red Indians
plus a few European colonists who weren't much
better than Indians.

They were almost right. The British colonies
along the Atlantic seaboard were only a hundred
years old or so. Most of the colonists were farmers,
who had all they could do to tame the wilderness
and fight off the Indians. There was little time to
give over to book-learning.

Yet there were cities, like Boston, New York, and
Philadelphia, where life was quite civilized and
where people could obtain considerable education.
Harvard University was founded in 1636, the College of William and Mary in 1693, and Yale University in 1702. As the 1700's progressed, the colonies
could number quite a few scholars among them-

selves: men who were skillful lawyers, and others who could write intelligent books.

But through all the years that the British colonies existed — from 1607, when Jamestown was settled, until 1776, when the colonies declared themselves independent — they could boast of only one important scientist. Only one in 169 years. That one scientist, however, was as good as any army, for he was Benjamin Franklin.

The Self-Made Man

6

BENJAMIN FRANKLIN was born in Boston, Massachusetts, on January 17, 1706. His father, Josiah Franklin, was an Englishman who had come to Massachusetts in 1682, just a year before Newton published his great book. Josiah brought his wife and three children with him. He had four more children after he arrived in America.

His wife died in 1689, and Josiah married a second time and went on to have ten more children by his second wife. Altogether, then, there were seventeen children and, of these, number fifteen was Benjamin. He was the tenth and youngest boy in the family. (This made the name Benjamin quite suitable, for, in the Bible, Benjamin was the youngest of Jacob's twelve sons.)

You can imagine it would have been difficult to arrange for an education for all these children, even if Josiah Franklin had been well-to-do, and he wasn't. Young Benjamin scarcely had any opportunity for schooling. When he was ten, he left school, and was put to work in a candle-maker's shop.

Candle-making, however, didn't suit Benjamin,

who dreamed of running off to sea. His father didn't want him running off, so he cast about for something else for the boy to do. Benjamin liked books and reading, so Josiah thought he would get his son a position that would involve reading. Benjamin's half brother James had a printing establishment and was putting out a successful newspaper. Why shouldn't Benjamin join him? At the age of twelve, therefore, Benjamin Franklin became a printer.

But Benjamin didn't take kindly to being ordered about by anyone, even by an older brother, and they quarreled bitterly. As the years passed, it struck Benjamin that perhaps he could do very well without his brother. After all, Benjamin knew he had abilities of his own. He wrote articles for the newspaper and they were quite good. Once or twice, when James got in trouble for some of the political articles he printed and had to remain out of sight for a while, Benjamin ran the paper altogether.

Consequently, Benjamin made up his mind to change jobs and get out from under his brother. This angered James, who saw to it that no other printer in Boston would hire Benjamin. There was nothing for the young man to do but leave Boston.

In October 1723, Benjamin Franklin, who was

now seventeen years old, left Boston for Philadelphia, and that city remained his home for the rest of his long life.

He arrived in Philadelphia with only one dollar in his pocket, but he got a job as a printer and showed himself to be capable and hard-working. The governor of Pennsylvania, at the time, was a man named William Keith. He took a liking to young Franklin and suggested he go to London to learn more about the printing trade.

Franklin traveled to London. He had very little money, but he got by, and spent two years learning about the great European world across the ocean.

He returned to Philadelphia in October 1726, and got another job as a printer. Within a year, however, he had enough money to set up a printing shop of his own. He was as capable and hard-working for himself as for others and the business did very well.

By 1729, he could afford to buy a newspaper called the *Pennsylvania Gazette*. It had been a failure as a newspaper, but Franklin changed that. He began to fill it with interesting, lively articles, and soon it was making money for him.

Franklin turned his hand to everything. He bought and sold books; he published books; he established branch printing offices in other cities. He started a club where intelligent young men could

gather and discuss the issues of the day. He started the first circulating library in America and the first fire-fighting company in Philadelphia.

His most successful business effort of all was an almanac, which he began to publish in 1732. He put out a new issue each year for twenty-five years.

The ordinary almanac publishes the calendar for the year, plus a great deal of information that is useful to farmers and sailors. It gives the dates for the different phases of the moon, the time of sunrise, sunset, moonrise, and moonset for each day, the time of high and low tide. It lists the eclipses that will take place, gives weather predictions, and so on. Such books are handy and usually sold well. (In fact such books still sell well.)

Franklin's almanac, however, was no usual one. It contained all the information that ordinary ones did, and it had something more as well. Franklin filled it with interesting and clever articles and also with many short and wise sayings, many of which he made up himself. For the most part, these sayings praised thrift and hard work.

The almanac (or "almanack," as the word was spelled in those days) was published by Franklin under the penname of "Richard Saunders." He called it *Poor Richard's Almanack.*

It sold very well, indeed. The farmers of the day simply gobbled it up. Many people took to repeat-

ing the maxims from the almanac. It was "As Poor Richard says . . ." and "Well, you know what Poor Richard says . . ." Here are some of the sayings of Poor Richard:

A word to the wise is enough.

God helps those who help themselves.

✷The sleeping fox catches no poultry.

✶Lost time is never found again.

Laziness travels so slowly that poverty soon overtakes him.

Diligence is the mother of good luck.

Little strokes fell great oaks.

Many a little makes a mickle [great deal].

He that goes a-borrowing, goes a-sorrowing.

✶ 'Tis hard for an empty bag to stand upright.

And, of course, the most famous of all the sayings of Poor Richard, and one that everyone knows is, ✶"Early to bed, and early to rise, makes a man healthy, wealthy and wise."

Benjamin Franklin was healthy and wise all his life, but *Poor Richard's Almanack* made him wealthy as well. By the 1740's, he had enough money to be able to retire.

In 1748, he made an arrangement with his partner by which Franklin was to receive an annual sum of money for his share in the business. The partner would then run the business and take what-

ever was left of the profits, after Franklin's annual sum was deducted.

Franklin then moved to the outskirts of the city and decided to devote himself to scientific research, as befitted a well-to-do gentleman of leisure in the Age of Reason.

This was not just an idle notion either. Franklin was quite an ingenious man who invented a number of useful gadgets. He was, in fact, the first great American inventor.

For instance, in those days houses were heated by fires in fireplaces. This was very wasteful of fuel for the hot air went straight up the chimney, and did not heat the house at all well. In fact, it stirred up a draft that brought in the cold air from outside the house. The only way for a family to get warm was to crowd round the fireplace, almost on top of the fire.

It occurred to Franklin that what was needed was an iron stove set out in the room. Inside that, a fire could be built. The metal would heat up and that would heat the air; the warm air would stay inside the room instead of vanishing up a chimney. As for the smoke, well, that could pass through a stovepipe into the chimney. The chimney would thus get rid of the smoke, but not the heat.

Franklin first built such a stove in 1739 or 1740, and it worked very well. Others had them built.

Franklin called it a "Pennsylvania fireplace," but everyone else called it a "Franklin stove." Franklin stoves have been very popular ever since, and even furnaces in the basements of modern houses are a kind of Franklin stove.

People suggested to Franklin that he patent the Franklin stove, so that he could charge a fee to any manufacturer who wanted to build and sell them. However, that would have raised the price of the stoves and Franklin did not wish to do that. He said that he enjoyed the inventions that other men had made, and, therefore, he should be willing to have others enjoy his inventions freely.

Here is another example. In 1757, while in London on business, Franklin happened to think of the way a moist finger, drawn round the top of a drinking glass, made a musical sound. The note changed with the size and thickness of the glass. Franklin amused himself, therefore, by constructing a device made out of glasses in the shape of hemispheres. There were about thirty-seven of these, of different sizes, which were fixed in a case. There was an arrangement whereby the glasses could be turned round and round by the action of a foot pedal. The glasses were kept moist and the fingers, too. As the rims of different glasses were gently rubbed, the different notes produced could be combined as music.

The glass harmonica, as it was called, was quite

popular for a while. Such composers as Beethoven and Mozart wrote little pieces to be played upon it. (Franklin wrote a musical composition himself; he could do almost anything.)

Franklin's ingenuity did not desert him in later life, either. More than once he thought of ways to make life easier for old men like himself. For example, many people, as they grow older, find that they have difficulty in seeing things close to their faces. This is the result of changes in the lens of the eye that comes with age, and for this reason, older people often have to wear reading glasses which adjust their sight to close vision. The same people may be nearsighted, too, and may have to wear glasses to help them see distant things. The glasses for one purpose won't suit the other, of course, and so it happens that older people may have to carry two pairs of glasses, one for distant vision and one for reading. Naturally, they would have to switch back and forth.

When Franklin reached the age where he needed two pairs of glasses, he found he was always reading and, therefore, always having to switch glasses. It drove him wild.

Finally, it occurred to him that this was not necessary. Why not one pair of glasses with double lenses? Each lens could be made up of two different pieces of glass. The upper half could be adjusted to

distant vision. The lower half could be adjusted to close vision.

Each half would have what spectacle-makers call a different "focal distance." Such double lenses would therefore be *bifocal glasses*. A person wearing bifocals would look through the upper halves of the lenses to see well at a distance. If he wanted to read, he merely lowered his eyes and looked through the lower half.

Benjamin Franklin had such glasses made for himself and was the first to wear bifocals. Millions of men and women have done so since, however, and have saved themselves a great deal of trouble.

Then, when Franklin was approaching his eight-

ieth year, he began to have some trouble with his library. It was a big one, and there were shelves near the ceiling. When he wanted a book from a high shelf, the logical thing to do was to get a little stepladder and climb up for it.

For a young man this was fine, but for an old man, who was getting unsteady on his legs, climbing a ladder could be dangerous. So Franklin devised a long stick, with a movable Y-shaped short stick attached to one end. He then attached a cord to the Y-stick. When he pulled the cord, the two parts of the stick came together. It was like a long-handled pair of pincers, or artificial hand, that could be worked from the ground.

With this instrument, he could reach up to the ceiling, if he had to. He could pluck a book off the high shelf and bring it down. When he was through, he could pinch the book in his wooden device, raise it up, and put it back on his high shelf.

Improved versions of the instrument are still used today in old-fashioned grocery stores. When the grocer wants a package from the top shelf, he uses Franklin's little gadget.

Franklin had many advanced scientific ideas, too. He was the first to notice that there was a band of warm water moving across the Atlantic. It wasn't until a century later that others began to realize the importance of the "Gulf Stream." He tried to

predict weather by noting the movement of storms, and favored daylight saving time as a means of saving fuel. Both notions eventually came to be important, but not for a hundred and fifty years. Franklin was that far ahead of other people of his time. But what really made Franklin famous the world over was his work with electricity.

In 1747, shortly after the Leyden jar was invented, Franklin received one from England. A friend of his, Peter Collinson, a London merchant who was a member of the Royal Society, sent it to him. Franklin was fascinated. In fact, it was his interest in electricity that was probably the final straw in persuading him to retire from business the next year.

Like other experimenters, Franklin could not resist playing tricks with the Leyden jar. One Christmas, for instance, he thought he would be very modern and kill his Christmas turkey with a shock from a group of Leyden jars. This was all right, except that Franklin accidentally got the shock and nearly killed himself instead of the turkey. However, he tried again, killed the turkey, then roasted it over a fire which he started by electricity from the same Leyden jars. Later, he proposed that all animals used for food be killed by electric shock, because that would be quicker and kinder than the usual methods.

But never mind the tricks. Once Franklin had his electrical device to play with, he began to do real wonders. He ended by outdoing all the electrical experimenters of Europe.

Positive and Negative

7

FRANKLIN performed some experiments that led him to agree with Du Fay. There were indeed two kinds of electricity: vitreous electricity and resinous electricity. Certain points bothered him, though. Where did the electricity come from? A piece of glass had no electricity to begin with, so it seemed. Then, after it was rubbed, it had electricity. Very well, where did that electricity come from?

Franklin decided to try an experiment. He asked two men to stand on cakes of wax. Each one was insulated from the floor so that any electric charge he received he would keep. One of the men was given a glass rod to rub. After he had rubbed it for a while, the glass rod would be electrified. Now the second man reached over and touched the glass rod, so that the electrical fluid it contained would pour into himself.

Just to keep things straight, let's call the first man the "Giving Man" because, after he rubbed the glass and formed the electricity, he gave it to the other man. The other man, who touched the

rubbed glass rod and received the electricity, we can call the "Receiving Man."

Naturally, Franklin expected the Receiving Man to be electrified, and he was. If a third man came along, standing on the ground (not on wax), and touched the Receiving Man's finger, there would be a spark, as electrical fluid ran through the third man and into the ground.

The odd part, though, was that the Giving Man was *also* electrified, even though he had not received any electricity. In fact, he had given electricity away. Yet when a third man, standing on the ground, touched the Giving Man's finger, there was a spark again. In fact, the spark obtained on touching the Giving Man looked just about like the spark obtained on touching the Receiving Man. They both seemed to have the same amount of electricity.

Franklin tried something else. After the Giving Man had rubbed the glass rod and passed the electricity on to the Receiving Man, he had the two men touch fingers. Since they were both electrified, perhaps there should have been no spark at all. But there *was* a spark. Not only that, but the spark was much brighter than when either man had touched the third man on the floor.

After the spark passed between the Giving Man and the Receiving Man, neither one was in the least electrified. Either one could touch a man on the floor and there would be no spark at all. The electricity in the Receiving Man had exactly neutralized the electricity in the Giving Man (or vice versa).

How was Franklin to explain all this? Franklin decided that electricity wasn't created out of nothing. It was in all objects all the time. However, all

objects, under ordinary conditions, contained the electrical fluid under the same pressure. If you touched anything there was no reason for the electrical fluid to flow from you to the object, or from the object to you. Therefore, nothing seemed to be electrified.

Suppose, though, you rub a glass rod. The rubbing, somehow, causes a little bit of the electrical fluid to pass from you into the glass rod. The glass rod would now have *more* electrical fluid than it normally possesses. This can be passed on to the Receiving Man who becomes electrified.

But when you rub a glass rod so that some of the electrical fluid passes from you into the glass rod, you end up with *less* electrical fluid than you should have. You are electrified, too.

If the Receiving Man, with too much electrical fluid, touches a man standing on the ground (who has an average amount), the fluid passes from the Receiving Man to the man on the ground. There is a spark.

If the Giving Man, with too little electrical fluid, touches a man standing on the ground (who has an average amount), fluid passes from the man on the ground to the Giving Man. Again there is a spark.

To be sure, the spark moves in different directions. It moves toward the grounded man, in the first case, and away from the grounded man, in the

second. However, the spark travels so quickly that it is impossible for anyone, however closely he watches, to see in which direction it moves. That is why both sparks seem the same. What happens then if the Receiving Man touches the Giving Man. Now a man with too much electrical fluid is touching a man with too little electrical fluid. The difference between them is twice as great as it would be if either one of them were touching a man on the ground, one with an average amount of fluid. That is why there is now a particularly bright spark.

When the spark has passed, the Receiving Man has lost his extra fluid, and the Giving Man has gained his missing fluid. Both now possess an average amount and neither is electrified.

So Franklin decided that though there were two kinds of electricity, this came about through the existence of only one electrical fluid, not two as Du Fay had thought.

What Du Fay had called "vitreous electricity" was simply a more than average quantity of electrical fluid. Franklin called that *positive electricity*. A glass rod, when it was rubbed, became *positively charged*.

Again, what Du Fay had called "resinous electricity," Franklin decided was only a less than average quantity of electrical fluid. This Franklin called

negative electricity. When Thales had rubbed his piece of amber over two thousand years before, it had become *negatively charged.*

Whenever electricity was formed by rubbing, then one object became positively charged, the other negatively charged. If glass was rubbed with silk, the glass gained a positive charge, the silk a negative one. If amber were rubbed with wool, the amber gained a negative charge, the wool a positive one.

This one-fluid theory of electricity was quickly adopted by scientists everywhere. To this very day we talk of positive and negative electricity. (In one way, however, Franklin had guessed wrong, but I will tell you about that at the end of the book.)

Once Franklin had his one-fluid theory of electricity worked out, he considered the Leyden jar. He decided that the reason it worked as it did, was that there was a negative charge on the metal foil inside the jar and a positive charge on the metal foil outside the jar. The glass in between, which would not conduct the electrical fluid, kept the two types of charge from neutralizing each other. For this reason, large charges could be built up, much larger than if there were no insulator between the two.

But if that were so, then why need the glass be in

the shape of a jar? Suppose a flat piece of glass were used, with tinfoil on both sides. A negative charge could be put on the tinfoil on one side, and a positive charge on the other, and you would have the effect of a Leyden jar, without a jar. This turned out to be correct.

Modern condensers, used to store considerable quantities of electricity, are all in the form of flat plates of conducting material with insulators in between. There is hardly any piece of electrical equipment that doesn't have this sort of condenser somewhere. Well, it was Franklin who introduced it.

Franklin conducted a set of experiments, in 1747, that were of great importance. They dealt with the effect of pointed objects on the electrical fluid. He began by taking an iron sphere, about three or four inches in diameter, and resting it on the mouth of a clean, dry bottle. In this way, it was insulated.

From the ceiling, he suspended a little cork ball by a silken thread. It, too, therefore, was insulated. The position and length of the silken thread were such that the cork ball just rested against the iron sphere.

Next he electrified the iron sphere by touching it with a charged Leyden jar. That meant that both

the iron sphere and the little cork ball that touched it were filled with negative electricity. Two objects, both filled with negative electricity, repel each other. (As Du Fay had shown, likes repel and unlikes attract.)

Consequently, when the iron sphere and cork ball were electrified, the cork ball sprang away and remained four or five inches away. The silken string no longer hung straight downward but, in defiance of gravity, hung at an angle.

Now it was possible for Franklin to tell exactly when he had drawn off the electricity from the iron sphere. If the electricity were drawn off in any way, the sure sign of this fact would be that the cork ball would no longer be repelled by the iron sphere. It would be pulled down toward the sphere, at once, by the force of gravity.

If Franklin touched the iron sphere with a conductor, such as his own finger, for instance, while he was standing on the ground, the electricity would shoot off the sphere and the cork ball would come down immediately.

Nor did he need to touch the sphere, actually. As I said in Chapter 5, air is not a perfect insulator. If a conductor approaches a charged body, there is a certain point where the thin layer of air between the conductor and the charged body will no longer insulate. The electricity leaps the gap and is gone.

When Franklin moved his finger or a rounded piece of metal near the charged iron sphere, the charge was lost when the air gap was about an inch. When that happened, there was the usual little spark and crackle.

Franklin found the situation quite different, however, when he used a sharply pointed conductor. He found that he could place a metal needle six or eight inches away from the charged sphere and cause it to lose its charge. He could tell that because the cork ball came down.

What's more there was no noticeable spark in the case of the sharp needle. But if he tried the experiment in the dark, he noticed a faint light gathering about the needle when it was still quite a distance from the sphere. As soon as that faint light was visible, the electric charge on the sphere was gone.

It seemed to Franklin that the sharp points drew the electrical fluid to themselves. He also decided that the sharp points cast off the electrical fluid. If he attached a needle to the iron sphere, he could not electrify that sphere. It was as though any electrical fluid entering the sphere ran silently, and without light, out of the metal point of the needle.

This set Franklin to thinking furiously. He had noticed the spark and crackle produced when an electric charge was taken off in the ordinary way.

Many had noticed that this was like a very tiny bolt of lightning and a very little peal of thunder. Franklin thought of that, too.

Could it be that, during thunderstorms, the earth and the clouds formed a huge Leyden jar? Were the clouds negatively charged, while the earth was positively charged? (Or vice versa?) Was the lightning the huge spark that evened things up for just a little while? Was the thunder the tremendous "crackle" that went along with the spark?

Several people had suggested this might be so, but Franklin did more than suggest. He thought he had a way to prove whether this suggestion was correct or not. The thought had come to him as a result of his experiments with pointed objects.

The Hammer of Thor

8

THE THUNDER and lightning, to which Franklin now raised his eyes in wonder, were beautiful, but they were also fearsome. Man, from his earliest days, had been in dread of the lightning flash. Suddenly the lightning strikes and there is no way of predicting where it will hit or what it will do. It may blast trees and set forests on fire. It may destroy houses and kill men.

Almost every set of myths has the lightning under the control of some powerful god. It is his weapon, his lance; with it, he slays his enemies.

The myths most familiar to us are those of the Greeks. The Greeks imagined that the lightning bolts were huge, gleaming, deadly swords that were forged over a fire, as human swords were. They thought that only the volcanoes were forges huge enough for such great swords as the lightning. In particular, they pointed to Mount Etna, which stands on the eastern shore of the island of Sicily, and was the largest volcano known to them.

Deep inside Mount Etna, the Greeks imagined,

the lightning-makers were to be found. These were three Cyclopes (sy-kloh'peez, meaning "round-eyes" in Greek), who were pictured as great giants with one round eye in the middle of the forehead. Their names were Brontes (bron'teez, "thunder"), Steropes (ster'oh-peez, "lightning"), and Arges (ahr'jeez, "brightness").

According to the Greek myths, the Titans ruled the universe in the early days. The chief of the Titans, Cronos, imprisoned the Cyclopes far underground, since they seemed too dangerous to be allowed to run free. The sons of Cronos, however, under the leadership of Zeus (zyoos), revolted against the Titans. For ten years, the war continued without sign of an end. Then Zeus went underground and liberated the Cyclopes. In gratitude, the giants made lightning for him. With the lightning bolts as his weapons, Zeus was able to defeat the Titans and become lord of the universe.

The Greeks thus believed lightning to be cast down upon the earth by Zeus, in order to terrify or punish those with whom he was angry. The Romans later considered Zeus to be the same god as their own Jupiter. They thought it was Jupiter who controlled the thunder and lightning. Sometimes they spoke of "Jupiter Fulminator" ("Jupiter, the lightning-hurler"), and sometimes of "Jupiter Tonans" ("Jupiter, the thunderer").

In the Norse myths, lightning also played an important role. The second most important of the Norse gods was called Thor by the Scandinavians and Donner by the Germans. Donner is still the German word for "thunder," so you can see at once that he must be involved with the lightning.

Thor was the strongest of the Norse gods and had flaming red hair. His weapon was a hammer named Mjollnir (myawl'ner, meaning "destroyer"). Thor never missed his mark when he threw Mjollnir. Whatever he aimed at, he hit; and whatever Mjollnir hit, it destroyed. What's more, after it was thrown, Mjollnir always returned to Thor's hand, so that it was always ready to throw again.

There's no doubt, then, that Mjollnir was really the lightning. Thor was lord of the lightning to the Teutonic tribes, as Zeus and Jupiter were to the Greeks and Romans.

The Romans named the fifth day of the week after Jupiter, and so the Teutonic tribes named it after Thor. To the Germans, the fifth day of the week is "Donnerstag," and to us, of course, it is "Thursday."

The ancient Hebrews developed a picture of God that was greater than those of the Greeks and the Teutons. The God of the Bible is absolute master of the universe in every way, and His word is enough.

It is not necessary for Him to fight enemies with the lightning. Still, in the more poetic portions of the Bible, the picture is sometimes drawn of the thunderstorm as a weapon of God.

In the 18th Psalm, for instance, the coming of God, in response to a call of distress, is described. The manner in which He strikes down His enemies is also described:

9 He bowed the heavens also, and came down: and darkness was under his feet.

10 And he rode upon a cherub, and did fly: yea, he did fly upon the wings of the wind.

11 He made darkness his secret place; his pavilion round about him were dark waters and thick clouds of the skies.

12 At the brightness that was before him his thick clouds passed, hail stones and coals of fire.

13 The Lord also thundered in the heavens, and the Highest gave his voice; hail stones and coals of fire.

14 Yea, he sent out his arrows, and scattered them; and he shot out lightnings, and discomfited them.

15 Then the channels of water were seen, and the foundations of the world were discovered at thy rebuke, O Lord, at the blast of the breath of thy nostrils.

The picture so drawn is surely that of a dreadful thunderstorm. Many Jews and Christians, in later times, could not help but feel that the lightning was

a particular weapon of God. When lightning struck a place or a person, it was God showing His anger with that place or person.

Lightning was particularly terrifying, too. Other dreadful things that happened struck many men. War and famine and disease killed thousands upon thousands, but lightning killed only a few. It made it look as though lightning were a personal punishment; it killed one particular person for his sins.

When a thunderstorm rose, then, and thunder rolled and lightning flashed, many people would hide in terror, thinking that their sins had found them out. They would expect a flash to come at any moment and put an end to them. Then, too, after the heathen peoples of Europe were converted to Christianity, there was still the memory of Zeus and his lightning, and of Thor and his hammer. The old gods were now considered to be demons, so many still felt that thunderstorms were under the control of such demons.

During the Middle Ages, therefore, there were often attempts to guard against lightning through prayer. Sometimes religious parades were held, and various holy objects were held high. In particular, church bells were rung, since it was felt that demons would have no power where such a holy sound was to be heard.

Indeed, the terror of lightning was very real.

But now Benjamin Franklin lifted his eyes to the heavens and decided that lightning was a natural force that followed natural laws. It was not the arrow of Zeus or the hammer of Thor, and neither was it under the control of demons. It was just the spark of a gigantic Leyden jar. He believed he would be able to prove it, too.

Franklin, as I explained, had found that pointed objects seemed to "draw the electric fire"; that is, they discharged an electrified body over a greater than usual distance. Therefore, in order to discharge the thunderclouds (if they really contained electricity), one would have the best chance if one used a long pointed object, and raised it as near as possible to the clouds. Franklin wrote about these ideas in letters to learned men in Europe.

Some European scientists took this most seriously. A Frenchman, Thomas d'Alibard (dah-lee-bahr'), on May 10, 1752, set up a pointed metal rod forty feet tall. During a thunderstorm, it was possible to draw sparks from the rod by placing a conductor near it.

Did this prove that lightning was electricity? Actually, it did, but the proof wasn't certain. Scientists weren't certain that the electricity really came from the thunderclouds, which were far, far overhead. Maybe it came from elsewhere, somehow.

While the scientists hesitated about this, Frank-

lin set about a much more dramatic experiment, which was to settle matters once and for all. He realized that the pointed rod would have to be quite close to the thundercloud, so that there would be no mistake about where the electricity came from. He suggested that such a rod be placed on top of a building.

At just this time, a new church was being built in Philadelphia, and it was Franklin's idea to place his pointed rod at the top of the very high spire of the church. While waiting, though, he got an even better idea. Why not use a kite? That would raise his pointed rod even higher than any church steeple.

It was during the month of June, 1752, when Franklin made ready. D'Alibard had done his work the month before, but there had been no time for news to cross the Atlantic yet, and Franklin had not heard of the Frenchman's experiment. There was no reason, therefore, for Franklin to be sure the experiment would work.

He was a little shy of flying kites in a thunderstorm for, after all, the experiment might not work, and then, he might find it difficult to explain why he was playing a child's game in the rain. (He didn't want to be laughed at. After all, who does?) So he kept his plan secret, telling only his son, who helped him get ready.

Franklin tied a pointed metal rod to the wooden

framework of the kite and attached a length of twine to it. This he attached to the cord which held the kite. Franklin felt that the pointed rod would draw the electricity out of the thundercloud. As soon as the cord of the kite was wet with rain, it would conduct the electricity down to himself. He supplied the end of the cord near himself with a conductor in the shape of an iron key.

Now there was one important thing left to do. There was no use in having the electricity enter himself. If it did, it would simply pass right through him and into the ground. It would disappear, and how would he test for it then?

Franklin therefore tied a strong silk string to the kite cord and held the cord by that silk string. During the storm he planned to stand under a shed so that he and the silk string would remain dry. The silk string would then be an insulator and any electricity picked up by the pointed rod might spread down the twine and cord and into the key, but would go no further.

Franklin and his son waited under the shed as the stormclouds gathered. The kite vanished into one of the clouds and then Franklin noted that the fibers of the kite cord were standing apart, as though all had the same electric charge and were repelling one another. There was electricity in the cord, he felt certain.

With great courage, he brought the knuckle of his hand near the key. After all, if lightning was electricity, it was certainly a great deal of electricity —enough to kill.

However, lightning had not struck the kite; electricity from the cloud was entering the point on the kite and pouring down to the key *without* lightning, so Franklin took the chance.

As his knuckle came close to the key, a spark leaped out. It was exactly the same spark Franklin had seen a hundred times when he worked with a Leyden jar. It made just the same crackling sound and it felt just the same when it met his hand.

Then Franklin went a step farther than D'Alibard. He had brought a Leyden jar with him. He touched the key to the Leyden jar and charged it! Now he had a Leyden jar full of electricity which he had drawn from the heavens, and it acted just like the electricity that men had been studying on earth.

The proof was complete. The lightning and the humble sparks produced by an electrical friction machine were one and the same. Both were electricity. One was a much larger spark than the other, but that was all. Franklin had played with the hammer of Thor and lived to tell the tale.

The Pointed Umbrella

9

WHEN THE NEWS of Franklin's experiment reached Europe, it created a sensation. Scientists and scholars hastened to repeat the experiment, and Franklin was shown to be correct. Franklin was elected a member of the Royal Society of London that same year.

(It was also found that Franklin's experiment was dangerous. In St. Petersburg, Russia, a Swedish professor, George William Richman, collected too much electricity. A spark sprang from the iron rod to his head and killed him at once.)

All the European gentlemen of the Age of Reason were now praising Franklin. His experiments were spoken of everywhere. The German philosopher, Immanuel Kant, hailed Franklin as "the new Prometheus," who had stolen fire from heaven. (Prometheus was a Titan in the Greek myths who, pitying mankind when they had first been created, stole fire from the sun and gave it to mankind, so that they might warm themselves and cook their food.) Kant lived in Koenigsberg, on the shores of

the Baltic Sea, by the way. He was next door to the
amber that had started it all, so many centuries ago.

But Franklin was not content merely to demon-
strate that lightning was electricity. If pointed rods
could discharge the clouds, they might be able to
keep the clouds from building up enough of a
charge to start a bolt of lightning. Or, if the lightning did start, it would strike the rod more easily
than anything else in the neighborhood. If the rod
were connected to conductors that led the electricity down to the ground, the lightning could do no
further harm.

What, then, if such a rod, or a group of them,
were placed on the tops of buildings? Would not
such a building be safe from lightning?

Benjamin Franklin announced this possibility in
the 1753 edition of *Poor Richard's Almanack*. Here
is what he had to say:

It has pleased God in His goodness to mankind, at
length to discover to them the means of securing their
habitations and other buildings from mischief by thunder and lightning. The method is this: Provide a small
iron rod (it may be made of the rod-iron used by the
nailers) but of such a length, that one end being three
or four feet in the moist ground, the other may be six
or eight feet above the highest part of the building. To
the upper end of the rod fasten about a foot of brass

wire, the size of a common knitting needle sharpened to a fine point; the rod may be secured to the house by a few small staples. If the house or barn be long, there may be a rod and point at each end, and a middling wire along the ridge from one to the other. A house thus furnished will not be damaged by lightning, it being attracted to the points, and passing thro the metal into the ground without hurting any thing. Vessels also, having a sharp pointed rod fix'd on the top of their masts, with a wire from the foot of the rod reaching down, round one of the shrouds to the water, will not be hurt by lightning.

Such rods as these suggested by Franklin were called "Franklin rods" by some and "lightning rods"

by others. In Great Britain, they are called "lightning conductors."

The idea was so simple that it almost seemed like trying to prevent lightning by muttering a charm or by burning incense. However, it had experimental backing behind it, and in the Age of Reason there was much respect for the new science.

Besides, what could anyone lose but a piece of iron and some wire? Even if it didn't work, you were no worse off; and if, on the other hand, it did, you might save your home from destruction.

Lightning rods began to rise over buildings in Philadelphia by the hundreds, then in Boston and New York. People began to notice that houses without lightning rods might be hit by lightning, but that houses with them usually weren't damaged by lightning, even when hit. The rods went up faster than ever. (Actually, the lightning rod isn't perfect protection, particularly if it is put up sloppily. Still it is a great deal better than nothing.)

Almost overnight, Franklin was not only a great scientist, he was the protector who had warded off the lightning. For the first time in history, one of the great dangers to mankind had been beaten. Old age and death still visited all humanity as they always had. So did famine and disease. (In Franklin's time, doctors had not yet learned to prevent or to cure a single important disease.) But the

lightning, at least, was beaten, and one deadly enemy was gone.

American colleges proudly honored their fellow countryman, who had provided a shield against the lightning. In July 1753, he was given an honorary degree by Harvard University. In September of that year, he received one from Yale. (Not bad for someone who had stopped his schooling at the age of ten.) Then, in November, Franklin was awarded the Copley gold medal, its greatest honor, by the Royal Society itself.

Even Louis XV of France (who, at that time, was an enemy of the American colonists) sent him a complimentary letter. The greatest European scientists and scholars knew of Franklin and considered him their equal, even if he was an American from the wilderness of the New World. Franklin was the only man in all of sprawling colonial America who had made a name for himself in the great world. Nor did his generosity fail, for just as Franklin had never patented the Franklin stove, so he never patented the Franklin rod. He gave it freely to the world, without any thought of making money out of it.

To be sure, Franklin's lightning rods met with some opposition. There were a number of people who felt that since lightning was cast down from

Heaven to punish sinners, it was wicked to try to put up rods to guard against God's punishment. In 1755, there was an earthquake that did some damage in Boston, and certain preachers claimed that this was because of God's anger at lightning rods.

Those who favored the lightning rod had several arguments on their side, also. In the first place, they held that if God really wanted to punish sinners, He could do it in spite of the lightning rods. It was foolish to think a little rod of iron was stronger than God.

On the other hand, if lightning was just a natural phenomenon, why was it wrong to protect oneself? The rain was sent by God, just as much as lightning was, and yet no one objected to the use of an umbrella to keep from getting wet. Well then, wasn't a lightning rod just a kind of pointed umbrella for use against lightning?

This certainly made sense. Still, even when lightning rods went up all around them, those in charge of churches hesitated. Priests and ministers hated to show a lack of confidence in God; surely they could depend on God to protect buildings that were holy to Him.

The trouble was that church spires were usually the tallest objects in town, and the objects nearest the clouds. It was easier for lightning to strike those spires than anything else in the vicinity.

Churches were, therefore, constantly being struck by lightning. About a dozen churches were struck by lightning each year in Germany alone.

So, one by one, churches also began to put up lightning rods. In Siena, Italy, the beautiful cathedral had been struck by lightning a number of times over the centuries. Each time, there had been considerable damage. In the 1760's, a lightning rod system was installed. People watched and waited. In 1777, lightning struck again, but it hit the rod, slid down the wires to the ground, and did the cathedral no injury whatever.

On the other hand, there was a church in Venice which was not protected by lightning rods. It wasn't believed necessary. The Venetian government was so sure a church was safe that it stored a hundred tons of gunpowder in the church vaults. In 1767, the church was hit by lightning, the gunpowder exploded, three thousand people were killed, and much of the city of Venice was destroyed.

After that, the arguments against lightning rods died down. People came to realize that, as Poor Richard had said, God helps those who help themselves.

Meanwhile, another dispute arose. Some people began to suggest that lightning rods with round

ends would be better than lightning rods with pointed ends. Why they should think this is puzzling, for all the experiments were on the side of pointed ends.

The argument was particularly strong in England during the late 1770's, and a scientific commission was appointed to look into the matter. It did so, and gave as its opinion that pointed ends were needed.

At this point, foolish, stubborn King George III took a hand. All he knew was that Benjamin Franklin had said pointed ends were correct, and that Benjamin Franklin was now a leader of the American rebels fighting against him.

He decided, therefore, to replace the pointed lightning rods on the palace, with others having round ends, just to show how much he hated Franklin. He ordered the Royal Society to announce that round ends were better than pointed ones.

The president of the Royal Society at the time was John Pringle, a Scottish physician who was an old friend of Franklin's. He was one of the greatest doctors of his time and the founder of military hygiene. He introduced methods of cleanliness into the army and greatly cut down the rate at which soldiers died of disease. He was the physician to various members of the royal family and, after 1774, he was physician to George III, himself.

It was old John Pringle who received the royal order to come out in favor of rounded ends. He faced the king angrily and said, "Sire, I cannot reverse the laws and operations of nature."

King George was a stubborn man, however, and he was determined to be greater than the laws of nature. He said that if Pringle did not do as he was told, he had better resign as president of the Royal Society. Pringle resigned at once.

But the laws of nature were stronger than the king after all. Eventually, the lightning rods over the palace were changed back to those with pointed ends. No one has ever dreamed of having any other kind since George III's day.

As for the poor King, he is, perhaps, not to be blamed very much. Some years after he had been beaten by Franklin and the Americans, he went mad. For the last thirty years of his long life, he remained mad, with only occasional brief spells of sanity. Perhaps he had never been entirely sane.

The Idea of Union

10

BUT EVEN while Franklin was engaged in his electrical experiments, he also entered politics. The colonies might be under the control of Great Britain, but there was still politics to get into. The British Parliament might tax the colonies, and control their commerce, and send over officials to act as governors and judges, but each of the thirteen colonies could, to a certain extent, decide on matters that concerned only itself.

This was, in some ways, rather like the situation today. The federal government, in Washington, D.C., controls the policies of the United States and each state within it. Each of the fifty states, however, has a legislature of its own and passes laws concerning matters that involve only that state.

Of course, there are important differences. In the United States today, the people of the different states vote for senators and representatives who go to Congress and guard their state's interests. The people of the different states also vote for the President, who is going to make the general decisions. In addition, there is a Constitution that keeps the

federal government from taking over too much con·
trol of the states.

In Colonial times, however, the people of the
American colonies could not vote for members of
the British Parliament. They could not count on
their own representatives in Parliament who would
protest against unfair taxes or against harmful trade
regulations.

Nor was there any definite agreement as to how
much self-government the colonies might have. The
British king could take over as much control as he
wanted. When the actions of a colony displeased
him (as they sometimes did), he could suspend that
colony's self-government altogether, if he wished
(and he sometimes did).

On the other hand, there were good points about
the British control, too. The British navy was the
strongest in the world. Without its protection, the
American colonies, with their long seacoast, might
have been subjected to attacks by pirates and by
ships of enemy nations.

Then there was danger in the fact that France
controlled Canada to the north of the colonies, and
all the Mississippi valley to the west. The colonies
occupied just a narrow strip between the Appalach-
ian mountains and the Atlantic coast, so they didn't
feel at all safe.

There weren't as many colonists in the French re-

gions as there were in the English colonies, but the French got along better with the Indians and used them as allies.

There had already been several wars with the French and the Indians. From 1689 to 1697, when William III was King of England, there had been King William's War. From 1702 to 1713, with Queen Anne ruling, there had been Queen Anne's War. And from 1743 to 1748, when George II was on the throne, there had been King George's War.

In all three cases, the end had been either a draw or a slight victory for the English. However, each time, there had been Indian massacres along the western and northern borders of the British colonies.

Now, in the 1750's, while Franklin was flying his kite, the French seemed to be getting ready for a fourth war, worse than all the rest.

No, indeed, British rule might be a bit annoying at times, but the colonists were only too happy to have the king's soldiers for protection against the French. What men like Franklin wanted, in fact, was *better* cooperation with the British.

This was hard to get in Pennsylvania, however, for several reasons. In the first place, Pennsylvania was a "proprietary colony." That is, it was first founded in 1682 by William Penn who, the year be-

fore, had received the land from King Charles II of England. Penn owned the land; he was its proprietor. Naturally, he didn't keep it all for his own personal use, but awarded tracts to settlers.

Just the same, Penn's descendants kept large estates for themselves, and felt they owned the colony and could do as they pleased with it. Sometimes, members of the Penn family served as governors of Pennsylvania. Even when others were governors, the Penns were usually in actual control.

Other landowners in Pennsylvania paid taxes to the colonial government, but the Penn family did not. What's more, nobody could make them do so but the king, and the Penns were careful to remain on good terms with the throne.

This angered and frightened many of the Pennsylvanians, for the trouble with the French and Indians was particularly bad in that colony. The French were slowly moving forts and trading posts eastward, along the Ohio River, into territory that the colonists considered to belong to Pennsylvania.

And yet Pennsylvania didn't seem to be able to move. For one thing, it was short of money because the Penns refused to pay taxes. For another, many of the colonists were Quakers — William Penn had been one — and Quakers didn't believe in wars and fighting. Also, many German settlers were coming into Pennsylvania, and they weren't as concerned

about the French as the colonists of English descent were. So Pennsylvania did almost nothing.

The first move, of what is now called the "French and Indian War," was, in fact, made by the colony of Virginia, which also laid claim to the Ohio Territory. Governor Dinwiddie, of Virginia, sent a young surveyor named George Washington to the Ohio Valley, in 1753. He was to try to persuade the French to leave the region, so as to prevent a war. Washington tried hard, but failed. The French felt they were winning, and they didn't want to quit.

The Virginians tried to build a fort at the point where the Allegheny and Monongahela rivers join to form the Ohio, but the French moved in and took it at once. The French finished the structure and called it Fort Duquesne (dyoo-kan'). Washington built another fort farther south, but the French defeated him and took that, too.

In 1755, the British decided that the French had grown too strong for the colonists to handle, so they sent in an army of their own. This army was headed by General Edward Braddock, a brave man and good officer, but one who hadn't the slightest idea of how to fight a proper battle against Indians.

He marched toward Fort Duquesne as though he were traveling through settled European countryside, instead of through the American wilderness.

Since he didn't bother sending out scouts to guard against ambush, he was easily ambushed by the French and Indians.

George Washington, serving on the General's staff, urged Braddock to order his army to fight from behind trees, Indian style. Braddock wouldn't hear of that, but insisted his soldiers stand in line, and fire in formation, just as though they were on a European battlefront.

The French and Indians didn't stand in line, however. They remained under cover. Their red coats made the poor British soldiers perfect targets and they didn't have a chance. They were mowed down. Braddock himself was killed. The British that escaped did so partly because some of Washington's Virginians carried on the fight Indian-style and kept the battle from being a total disaster.

Things looked bad for the colonists in the early 1750's, especially for the Pennsylvanians, yet, through all this, the Penns refused to budge.

In 1748, Benjamin Franklin had been elected to the Philadelphia city council. In 1750, he had moved up to the Pennsylvania assembly. (Each year, until 1763, he was to be re-elected to the assembly.)

His reputation as a wise and skillful man of business caused him to be appointed deputy postmas-

ter-general for all the colonies in 1753. Nor did
Franklin prove a disappointment. The post office
had been losing money each year. Once Franklin
took over and began to run it honestly and effi-
ciently, it started to show a profit at once.

As a member of the Pennsylvania assembly,
Franklin was a ringleader of those colonists who
opposed the do-nothing attitude of the Penns. He
fought hard to persuade Pennsylvania to establish
a kind of volunteer army for the protection of the
colony. He was also one of those appointed to try
to reach a settlement with the Indians in the western areas of Pennsylvania.

Even more important Indian negotiations were
in the wind, however. The most powerful Indian
group in the colonial territories were the Iroquois
Nations of central New York State. They were the
only important Indian federation that was completely against the French. It was important to
form a strong alliance with them, since war with
the French now seemed certain.

Therefore, the year before Braddock's defeat, the
British government called representatives of the
Iroquois Nations and of the colonists to consult in
Albany, the capital of the colony of New York.
Seven of the thirteen colonies were represented:
New Hampshire, Massachusetts, Connecticut,
Rhode Island, New York, Pennsylvania, and Mary-

land. On June 19, 1754, the Albany Congress, as it was called, met. One of the Pennsylvania delegates was Benjamin Franklin.

This was a turning point in his life. His electrical experiments were done. He had flown his kite and had invented the lightning rod. The rest of his life was devoted to the cause of the colonies. Not just to Pennsylvania, his own colony, but to all the colonies.

There were, after all, thirteen separate colonies. The first to be founded had been Virginia, in 1607; the thirteenth was Georgia in 1733. Each had its own assembly and its own laws. The different colonists considered themselves Virginians, Pennsylvanians, New Yorkers, and so on. They had disputes among themselves over boundaries and trade. They did not at all feel as though they were one group of people.

To Franklin, though, it seemed as though this were wrong. All the vast territory controlled by the French was under single control, and if the British colonies squabbled among themselves they would surely be destroyed. But why should they squabble? They were all occupied by people who were mostly of English descent and who spoke English. They had the same traditions, the same interests, the same enemies. Why not get together?

Franklin was the first person in American his-

tory to suggest this idea of union. When the Albany Congress finished its first order of business and made an alliance with the Iroquois Nations, Franklin felt it was time for an even bolder move. He asked for the floor and made a startling proposal, which he called "A Plan for a Union of the English Colonies in America."

He suggested that the colonies join under a president, who was to be appointed by the British king. The colonists could vote for a "great council," to which representatives of all the different colonies would be sent. Franklin outlined the powers that the president would have and those that the great council would have.

Had this plan been accepted, the history of the colonies might have been changed, and we might be living in a different world now. But it wasn't accepted. The British government turned it down because they felt the great council of the colonists would have too much power. The colonies turned it down, too, because they felt the president, appointed by the king, would have too much power. So it came to nothing.

And yet, thirty-five years later, it was to come true. The idea of union which Franklin had had was to come to pass. It came only after a war and after the colonies had separated from Great Britain, but it came.

Years later, the French writer Honoré de Balzac thought of this and said that, in addition to all his other inventions, Franklin had also invented the United States of America.

Failure in England

11

WITH FRANKLIN'S plan for union defeated, and with Braddock's army defeated the next year, it was time for strong measures. Those Pennsylvanians who wanted to take action against the French sent Franklin to England to carry on the fight against the disastrous policies of the Penn family.

Franklin arrived in England in 1757. (It was at that time that he invented the glass harmonica I mentioned in Chapter 6.)

He found himself a famous man in the mother country. Several universities awarded him honorary degrees, one coming even from famous old Oxford. He met old friends to whom he had written concerning his electrical experiments. There was Peter Collinson, who had sent him his first Leyden jar, ten years before. There was John Pringle, too, who was to be forced to resign his presidency of the Royal Society, fifteen years later, because the foolish King wanted to spite Franklin.

Franklin also met a Unitarian minister named Joseph Priestley, during his English stay. As a re-

sult, Priestley became interested in science, and began to experiment on his own. He studied gases and discovered the one we now call oxygen. This was one of the important steps that led to the founding of modern chemistry.

Twenty years after that discovery, Priestley was to get into trouble because he was sympathetic to the French revolutionaries. Eventually, he decided it would be safest to leave Great Britain and emigrate to the country of his old friend, Benjamin Franklin — a country which was now independent.

Priestley did so in 1794, and became the first of many scientists who, in later years, were to seek the freedom of the United States. Priestley spent the last ten years of his life in Pennsylvania.

While Franklin was in London, the tide of war began to turn. William Pitt was the strongest and ablest political leader in the land, but he was an enemy of King George II (grandfather of George III), and so he was kept out of power.

However, the French victories had made the situation so serious that the King could not hold out. In June 1757, William Pitt became Prime Minister, and the British began to fight in earnest. In 1758, the British captured Fort Duquesne, and thus avenged Braddock. The British changed the name to Fort Pitt, in honor of the Prime Minister,

and, later, the great city of Pittsburgh grew up on that site.

In 1759, the British general James Wolfe, led an army into Canada, where he besieged and finally captured the city of Quebec. From that moment on, French defeat in North America seemed certain. (At the same time, other British forces were defeating France in India.)

With victory in sight, the war became popular among the British, and Franklin became even more popular because he had always been in favor of the colonies fighting strongly with the British. The Penns, on the other hand, lost popularity because they had not contributed to the war. In 1760, therefore, the Penn family reluctantly decided they had better agree to pay some taxes.

Meanwhile, the British government was considering what it might demand of France when it came to make peace. Some influential government leaders cast their eyes on certain French islands in the West Indies, such as Guadeloupe. This island produced sugar, rum, and molasses, and in those days these were important trading items. It seemed more important to get such islands than to get Canada, which most British thought of as just an empty frozen waste, anyhow.

That didn't suit Franklin at all, however. If the

French were left in Canada, they would still be a danger to the colonies. There would always be the chance of a war of revenge. He wrote a pamphlet called "The Interest of Great Britain considered with regard to her Colonies," pointing out the advantages of owning Canada.

This helped to persuade the British government to change its mind. When the peace treaty with France was signed in 1763, the British took Canada, and it has stayed subject to the British crown ever since — though it is now a completely self-ruling nation. As for Guadeloupe, that was allowed to remain French, and it is still French to this day. Perhaps, then, we might say that Franklin invented the Dominion of Canada, as well as the United States of America.

Franklin returned to Philadelphia on November 1, 1762, the year before the peace treaty had been signed. However, everyone knew how things were to turn out, and Franklin was greeted as a hero.

But it wasn't a case of everyone living happily ever after, for new troubles developed. With the French finally defeated, a group of Indian tribes in the Ohio region united under a chief named Pontiac, to carry on a new war against the colonies. A

number of forts were captured by the Indians, but Fort Pitt held out and finally, in late 1763, the Indians were defeated.

But then worse came. The new governor of Pennsylvania was John Penn, one of the Penn family. With the war safely over, he went back on the agreement to have the Penn estates pay taxes.

Franklin was angry indeed. He decided there

was no use trying to deal with the Penn family at all. The only way out was to end the proprietorship altogether. Old King Charles II had given Pennsylvania to the Penns, eighty-three years before. Now the new king, George III — he had come to the throne in 1760 — could take it away and make Pennsylvania a "royal colony."

In November 1764, Franklin sailed once more for England in order to persuade George III to do this.

But Franklin was to find that things had changed. The war with France had ended in a great victory for Great Britain, but it had also been expensive, and the government needed a good deal of money. The British argued that much of the war had been fought in the colonies and the colonies had benefited by it. They had received new territory west of the Appalachians, and their dangerous enemy, France, was gone. Why shouldn't the colonists pay their share of the expense of the war, then?

This seemed to make sense to the British, so, in 1765, they passed what is called the Stamp Act. The colonists were supposed to buy stamps to place on newspapers and magazines and on all sorts of legal documents, such as marriage licenses and bills of sale. The newspapers and legal documents could not be used without the stamps, and the stamp money would go to the British government. It

wasn't much of a tax and it seemed reasonable enough to the British.

The colonists took a completely different view. They felt that the British had been fighting the French for their own safety, and for a larger share of the trade of the world. The colonists felt that they themselves had done their own full share of fighting in North America and didn't have to be beholden to anybody.

In addition, the colonists felt it was unfair to be subject to taxes when they had no representatives of their own in Parliament to argue the matter. In Massachusetts, James Otis said, "Taxation without representation is tyranny," and that became a colonial slogan.

Since the colonists no longer had France to fear, they felt free to argue with the mother country.

The various colonies got together and simply refused to buy the stamps. They treated the tax collectors roughly and boycotted British goods.

At first Franklin felt the colonists ought to accept the Stamp Act. He was a loyal subject to the King, and he didn't want the King to grow angry with the Americans just when it was important to get his support against the Penn family. However, when Franklin saw how high colonial feeling was running, he realized there was nothing to do but try to per-

suade the British to repeal the tax. He argued the case even before Parliament and, in 1766, the Stamp Act was repealed, partly through his influence.

Franklin was now more popular than ever. Other colonies, besides Pennsylvania, wanted him to represent their interests in Great Britain. He became an agent for Georgia, in 1768, for instance, and for Massachusetts, in 1770. He visited Scotland, Ireland, Germany, even his recent enemy France, and was greeted with enthusiasm everywhere.

However, George III, that stubborn, foolish man, never forgave the colonists for forcing his government to give in on the Stamp Act. And he never forgave Franklin either.

The British government kept on trying to impose other taxes (without representation) on the colonies. They decided that the trouble with the Stamp Act was that it had been a "direct tax." However, it had always been agreed that Great Britain could regulate the trade of the colonies, so the government raised the duties that the colonists would have to pay on a variety of imported materials. This was considered an "indirect tax" and therefore all right.

But the colonists didn't think it was all right at all. They kept on fighting any taxation without rep-

resentation and, in Great Britain, Franklin kept arguing that case very skillfully.

Finally, in 1773, the British removed all taxes except a single tax on tea. They made this an extremely small one. This was intended as a trap, and it might have worked, if the British had been clever enough to try it first. Now it was far too late. The colonists saw the trap.

If the colonists agreed to accept even one small tax, they would be admitting that the British government could tax them without American representation in Parliament. Once that was admitted, the British would consider themselves to have the right to add on any further taxes they wanted to. Consequently, the tea tax was bitterly fought by the colonists.

In November, ships carrying tea arrived at Boston and other ports, but the Americans would not allow the tea to be unloaded. In Boston, the angrier colonists wanted more than that. They wanted a real fight. So, disguised as Indians, a group of them boarded the ships in Boston harbor on December 16, 1773, and threw the tea overboard. This was the famous Boston Tea Party.

The Boston Tea Party was the last straw, as far as the British government was concerned. They prepared to put the city under martial law and fill it

with British soldiers. They called Franklin before the privy council in January 1774, insulted him, fired him from his job as deputy postmaster-general, and threatened him with arrest.

Franklin had to leave England. As a loyal British subject, he had done his best to keep the British government from foolishly driving the colonies to rebellion. He had failed!

Now he had no choice but to join the rebelling colonists, even though he knew that, if the colonial cause failed, he would be hanged as a traitor.

Success in France

12

WITH THE BRITISH hand hanging heavy over the rebellious Bostonians, the colonial leaders thought they had better unite. Twenty years before, Franklin had spoken of a union of colonies against the French. Now it seemed there would have to be one against the British.

In September 1774, representatives of twelve of the thirteen colonies (Georgia was not included) gathered in Philadelphia. This was the First Continental Congress, and it sat for almost two months. It drafted a petition to the King, explaining the colonial position. George III, however, was determined not to give in, and the petition came to nothing.

In April 1775, the first shots were fired at Lexington and Concord, in Massachusetts, and at once delegates were chosen for a Second Continental Congress. This met on May 10, 1775, and remained in session for a year and a half. With guns shooting, there came to be heard talk of independence, of breaking away from Great Britain altogether.

Talk of independence became especially impor-

tant after the appearance, in early 1776, of a pamphlet called "Common Sense." This was written by an Englishman named Thomas Paine, whose burning words fired those who read him.

Paine owed his position to Franklin. He had been scribbling away in London, without much success, when Franklin met him. Franklin was impressed with Paine's writing ability and, in 1774, gave him letters of introduction to influential men in the colonies. Paine's fiery pamphlets were to keep hope alive in American hearts during the darkest days of the Revolution.

Georgia had joined the Second Continental Congress, completing the full roll call of the thirteen colonies. However, there was still Canada to be heard from. The Congress sent three men, one of them Franklin, to Canada to try to get the Canadians to join the other colonists.

It was odd. Fifteen years before, Franklin had helped make Canada British. Now he was to attempt to turn her away from Great Britain. This time he failed. The British moves against Boston seemed to favor Canada. For instance, the boundaries of Canadian territory had been extended southward to the Ohio River. Canada, therefore, was content with British rule. Furthermore, the French in Canada still had no love for their old ene-

mies, the American colonists, and would not join them. (There were many men of French descent in Canada, even though the British had taken over. Their French-speaking descendants live in the Province of Quebec to this day.)

Franklin returned to Philadelphia in time to take part in the final decision to declare the colonies "free and independent states."

On June 10, 1776, the Congress appointed a committee of five men to draw up a Declaration of Independence. These were Thomas Jefferson of Virginia, John Adams of Massachusetts, Benjamin Franklin of Pennsylvania, Roger Sherman of Connecticut, and Robert R. Livingston of New York.

Jefferson was selected by the committee to do the actual writing, but Franklin went over the result and made some corrections. Independence was voted on July 2, but the Declaration itself was adopted on July 4. It is July 4 that is now celebrated as Independence Day.

This was the end of any hope for peace. There was no turning back. Various men put their names to the document, one after the other, knowing the danger. If the Americans lost, every man whose signature was there would surely be executed for treason. John Hancock of Massachusetts signed first. He did so in a large hand, "so that King George can read it without his spectacles." Charles

Carroll of Maryland was teased by other signers, and told that there were a number of men with his name in his state, so that he might be safe. The King would not know which one it was. For that reason, Carroll signed himself "Charles Carroll of Carrollton," to make sure there would be no mistake.

Someone said, "Now we must all hang together," for any disunity would be fatal. And Franklin said solemnly, "Most assuredly. Or we shall all hang . . . separately."

It was all very well to sign declarations, however, but Americans could not fight without ammunition and supplies. The Battle of Bunker Hill had shown that no soldiers could win without gunpowder. There was only one place to get gunpowder, and that was from the old enemy, France.

And there was only one man to send to France — Benjamin Franklin. He had been an enemy of France, and had moved heaven and earth to defeat her less than twenty years before, but he was the indispensable man just the same.

The French knew him, you see. He was the only American they knew. What's more, the French aristocrats of the Age of Reason admired him and considered him a hero. To them, Franklin was the man whose kite had brought down electricity from

the heavens and whose rod spread out a protection against the lightning.

In September 1776, he was chosen, as one of a committee of three, to travel to France. Franklin was an old man now; he had just turned seventy. He had traveled back and forth across the Atlantic a number of times and the trip, in those days, took two months and was difficult. His wife was dead; his only living son — the one who had helped him in his great kite experiment — had turned "Tory" and was fighting on the side of the King.

So life was hard for him in a number of ways. And yet, Franklin knew he had to work for his country. Once again, he made ready to cross the Atlantic and, in December 1776, he arrived in France.

He was greeted like a hero. He had been elected a member of the French Academy of Sciences four years earlier and now French scholars rushed to meet him.

Franklin deliberately dressed very simply, like a Quaker. He didn't wear a wig, or powder, or a sword. He carried a stout staff instead. The French aristocrats were enchanted with this simplicity. Franklin was particularly popular with the fashionable ladies of French society.

The French aristocrats even knew all about Poor Richard, for some of the maxims had been trans-

lated into French. It was odd that the aristocrats should be so taken with proverbs praising thrift and industry. They were extravagant and lazy themselves, and that was to help destroy them a little over ten years later.

However, they applauded Franklin as "Bonhomme Richard" (boh-num'ree-shahr'), wherever he went. In French "bonhomme" is an expression used for a common man of the people. That seemed to fit old Franklin and was as close as the French wished to get to the phrase "Poor Richard."

The French scholars and aristocrats began to put pressure on the government to help the struggling Americans. Actually, they were really interested only in helping Franklin, for the aristocrats knew very little about the colonies. They only knew Franklin and his kite — but that was enough for them.

A bust was being prepared of Franklin, while he was in France, and the French statesman Anne Robert Jacques Turgot (tyoor-goh') was chosen to write the inscription.

Turgot, himself, had been almost as wise a Frenchman as Franklin was an American. Turgot had been in French politics for most of his life and, in 1774, when Louis XVI became King of France, he was made Minister of Finance.

These finances were in terrible shape, which was

one of the reasons why France couldn't really afford to help the Americans. In order to improve the finances, Turgot saw that there would have to be many reforms in taxation and in the French system of government.

However, in order to make those reforms, he would have to see to it that the aristocracy paid taxes. He would have to stop graft and extravagance. He tried to do so, but the aristocracy turned against him and forced the King to discharge him in 1776. Had they been more sensible, and had they let Turgot carry through his reforms, the French Revolution might have been prevented. The aristocrats might have saved their heads. Turgot spent the last five years of his life in retirement and did not live to see the French Revolution.

In 1778, then, it was Turgot who wrote the inscription on the bust of Franklin. He wrote it in Latin, but, translated into English, it reads: "He snatched the lightning from the sky and the scepter from tyrants."

That was how the French felt. They had watched Franklin snatch the lightning from the sky and now they were eager to help him snatch the scepter from the tyrant, George III. Of course, the day would soon come when their own King, Louis XVI, would be called a tyrant, and his scepter, too, would be snatched away, and very bloodily. That was in the

future, though, and the French aristocrats weren't looking into the future.

When the news came, toward the end of 1777, that British General Burgoyne had surrendered at Saratoga, that was all the aristocrats needed. It showed that the Americans could win. Even the cautious Count Vergennes could resist no longer.

In February 1778, even though Washington's army at Valley Forge was at the edge of ruin, the French discarded caution. They signed a treaty of alliance with the United States. Instead of helping secretly, they now began to help openly and, of course, that meant war with Great Britain.

In March, Franklin was received by King Louis and Queen Marie Antoinette. They, too, admired him as the hero of the kite.

Even after the treaty of alliance was signed, there were problems. The war dragged on for years and more and more money — money that the French government did not really have — was needed. Franklin kept persuading the French to get the money somehow, to ship supplies, to send a fleet and an army.

One French gift was particularly important in establishing a proud American tradition. The Americans had no real navy and Great Britain had the strongest navy in the world. Nevertheless,

American sailors put up a strong fight in whatever ships they could get. They raided British merchant ships to seize their cargoes, much as two hundred years before, the English had raided Spanish merchant ships.

The most daring of the American sea captains was John Paul Jones, a Scotsman by birth. Throughout the war, the British navy never managed to catch him. However, political opposition back in the United States kept him from taking command of American activities on the sea. He couldn't even get a decent ship. Finally, he appealed to the French, and King Louis let him have an old beat-up vessel. It wasn't much good, but it was far better than nothing. Jones gave it a new name, the *Bonhomme Richard,* in honor of Franklin.

On September 23, 1779, the *Bonhomme Richard* met two British warships in the North Sea, off the east coast of England. One was the *Serapis,* the other the *Countess of Scarborough.* The *Serapis* was much stronger than the *Bonhomme Richard* and in the three and a half hour fight that followed, the rickety American ship was nearly blown to pieces.

The captain of the *Serapis* cried out across the water, "Do you give up?"

John Paul Jones shouted back furiously, "I have not yet begun to fight."

A few moments later a grenade from the *Bonhomme Richard* exploded some of the ammunition stored on the *Serapis* and that damaged the larger ship badly. The American guns that were left fired furiously and it was the *Serapis* that was finally forced to surrender.

But the *Bonhomme Richard* was about done. The American sailors had just enough time to board the *Serapis* and turn to watch their own ship sink. They sailed the *Serapis* to a French port and safety.

The exciting fight and victory of the *Bonhomme Richard,* and John Paul Jones's immortal defiance, established the tradition of victory for the American navy. It was to keep the tradition of victory ever afterward. And at the very head of that tradition is the name of "Poor Richard."

In 1781, Cornwallis surrendered at Yorktown to an army of French and Americans. Even George III could not continue the war after that. The war had grown too unpopular in England, and George III was just as unpopular. If he tried to continue, he might lose his throne altogether.

It remained to negotiate the peace. After Yorktown, Franklin was appointed a member of the commission that arranged the treaty of peace with England. On September 8, 1783, the document was signed at Versailles in France.

Franklin's kite had gone far to win the revolution. Great Britain had lost a war for the first (and only) time in modern history. The United States was a new nation, ruling from the Atlantic Ocean to the Mississippi River, over all the territories that lay between British Canada on the north and Spanish Florida on the south.

Franklin stayed on in France as the American minister, more popular than ever. More than ever he was looked upon as a great and wise scientist and philosopher.

In those days, an Austrian physician named Friedrich Anton Mesmer was taking French society by storm. Mesmer claimed he could cure diseases by something he called "animal magnetism." He made mysterious passes with his hands and tried other kinds of mumbo-jumbo.

Magnetism had nothing to do with it, of course. What Mesmer was doing was hypnotizing his patients, and having them think that that cured them. It is indeed possible to cure some ailments in this fashion, ailments that arise from some mental disorder. In 1778, Mesmer came to Paris and, in this way, cured some people with such disorders.

However, hypnotism cannot cure diseases that are caused by physical troubles, by germs or by tissue breakdown. (Germs had scarcely been heard of in

those days.) Therefore, some people were not cured, and they complained about Mesmer to the authorities.

The French government appointed a commission to investigate Mesmer's methods, and one of the members of the commission was Benjamin Franklin. Franklin's decision — with which the other members agreed — was that there was no such thing as "animal magnetism," and that Mesmer's methods were fake.

That was the end of Mesmer. He retired to Switzerland, where he spent the last thirty years of his life in obscurity. A whole century was to pass before the fakery was knocked out of Mesmer's work, and hypnotism came to be of actual use in medicine.

Finally, in 1785, the American government agreed to accept Franklin's resignation, and the old man left France. He stopped off in England, where he met his son (who, as a Tory, could not return to the United States) and forgave him.

Franklin reached Philadelphia in September 1785, after having been absent for nine years. He was now only a few months short of eighty years of age, and he was standing on the peaceful, free, and independent soil of a new nation, the United States of America.

The Nation Completed

13

THE PENNS no longer governed Pennsylvania, of course. Their rule had come to an end in 1776. During the Revolutionary War, Pennsylvania was governed by an executive council, with a president who was elected each year.

In 1785, when Franklin returned from France, he was promptly elected president of the executive council. He was re-elected in 1786, 1787, and 1788. This position was equivalent to that of governor of the state.

Meanwhile, the new nation was not having an easy time of it. The various states of the Union were not really united. Each state had been a separate colony, governing itself as much as Great Britain would allow. Now that they had gotten rid of Great Britain, they didn't want any other kind of interference.

The Continental Congress still sat, and it was supposed to rule the nation. There was even an "Articles of Confederation" which the states had approved in 1781. This was a set of rules that indicated how the Continental Congress was to govern.

Unfortunately, the rules were pretty poor, and the Continental Congress had so little power it could do nothing useful. For instance, it had no power to tax the states. (The states had fought against outside taxation from the British and now they wanted no other kind of outside taxation, either.) The Continental Congress could request voluntary contributions of money, but they were hard to get. The states might promise money, but they didn't always deliver.

Without gold or silver to back it, the paper currency put out by the Continental Congress during the war couldn't be exchanged for coin. It was worthless. (We still say something "isn't worth a Continental," when we mean it isn't worth anything at all.)

The states bickered among themselves, too. They tried to set up tariffs against one another. On a couple of occasions, they even threatened to fight. It seemed to many men in the country that this could not be allowed to go on. Sooner or later, the states would fall apart and set themselves up as separate little countries. They would try to protect themselves against their neighbors by making alliances with this European nation or that. Soon they would fall into the grip of Great Britain again, or perhaps become French puppets.

It was just as it had been for the signers of the

Declaration of Independence. Either states were going to hang together or they would hang separately.

One of those who favored a strong central government was James Madison of Virginia. In 1786, he arranged a meeting of representatives from the various states, in order that they might come to some agreement on trade policies. The meeting is called the "Annapolis Convention," because it was held in Annapolis, the capital of Maryland, on September 11, 1788.

Only five states sent delegates, however. These were New York, New Jersey, Pennsylvania, Delaware, and Virginia, so nothing important could be done.

But James Madison was there, and another man, Alexander Hamilton of New York, who also favored a strong central government. They decided that there was no use talking about trade alone. The whole structure of the government had to be changed. The Articles of Confederation just wouldn't do.

The one thing the Annapolis Convention did, then, was to put out a resolution, written by Alexander Hamilton, for another meeting of representatives from the states. This one was to meet the next

year in Philadelphia to consider reorganizing the government from top to bottom.

The meeting was held, indeed, and this time it was the real thing. It met on May 25, 1787, and delegates attended from every state but Rhode Island. It was the most important meeting held in the history of the United States, for it produced the Constitution. Under that document, the nation finally developed a practical central government.

Almost two centuries have passed since then, and the United States is still run according to the document drawn up at that Constitutional Convention.

Alexander Hamilton and James Madison were the leading spirits of the meeting. George Washington served as president of the convention. And, representing Pennsylvania, there was old Benjamin Franklin, in his eighty-second year.

It was not an easy convention. There were many disputes over the form the Constitution should take. Several times it looked as though the convention would break up; and if it had, the young United States might have fallen apart before it had really gotten started.

Fortunately, the situation was saved each time by a compromise. Franklin's wisdom and tact helped calm tempers and make the compromises possible.

Eventually, on September 17, 1787, the Constitution was approved by the convention.

Thirty-nine men from twelve states—all but Rhode Island—signed the Constitution. Eleven years before, fifty-six men had signed the Declaration of Independence.

These two documents are the most respected in the nation's history and only six men signed both. One was Roger Sherman of Connecticut and another George Read of Delaware. The other four were delegates from Pennsylvania: James Wilson, George Clymer, Robert Morris—and Benjamin Franklin.

The Continental Congress accepted the Constitution and forwarded it to the states. The first state to ratify the Constitution was Delaware, on December 7, 1787. Pennsylvania, however, under the influence of Franklin, was a quick second, for it ratified the Constitution on December 12. New Jersey followed on December 19.

In the next two months, Georgia, Connecticut, and Massachusetts signed. Maryland ratified in April of 1788, and South Carolina in May. That made eight states. The states had agreed that the Constitution would become the law of the land if two-thirds of the states approved. That meant at least nine states out of the thirteen.

The honor of being the ninth fell to New Hampshire, which ratified the Constitution on June 21, 1788. On that day, it became, officially, the Constitution of the United States. Virginia ratified as the tenth state on June 25th, and New York as the eleventh on July 26th.

The Constitution provided that the government be headed by a President chosen by an electoral college. There was no argument as to who the first President should be. George Washington was chosen unanimously. On April 30, 1789, George Washington was inaugurated as the first President of the United States, taking his oath in New York City.

Benjamin Franklin, now turning eighty-four, had lived to see his old plan for a union of the colonies, which he had proposed at the Albany Convention thirty-five years before, come true. There was such a union. There was a Congress, elected by the people. There was a President, too, not appointed by a British King, to be sure, but also elected by the people, through an electoral college.

The great structure was almost complete. North Carolina had ratified on November 21, 1789. Only stubborn little Rhode Island held out, but for a good reason. She felt there should be added safeguards to the Constitution. These would prevent the central government from endangering the liber-

ties of the states and the people. Other states felt the same, and it had been agreed to supply the Constitution with amendments to make sure of this.

In September 1789, a group of such amendments, now called the Bill of Rights, were sent to the states for ratification.

Meanwhile, Benjamin Franklin, in the last days of his life had turned his attention to another problem of liberty. The Declaration of Independence said, "All men are created equal."

Surely this meant what it said, and liberty must be for all men. (And Franklin should know what it meant, for he had helped draw up the Declaration.) Yet there were men and women in the United States who were not considered "equal," but were held in slavery. They were the Negroes.

This seemed wrong to Franklin, and he served as president of the Pennsylvania Society for Promoting the Abolition of Slavery. On February 12, 1790, he signed a petition addressed to Congress, requesting action on the problem. It was his last public act.

On April 17, 1790 in his eighty-fifth year, Benjamin Franklin died.

The nation he had helped bring into existence, with his kite that had brought down the electrical fire from heaven, lived on. Rhode Island finally ratified the Constitution on May 29, 1790, and the

Bill of Rights was adopted on December 15, 1791. The nation was completed.

The United States grew and prospered. It even survived a great and bloody Civil War brought on by the very question of slavery which had disturbed Franklin's final months of life. It stands now as the richest and most powerful nation on the earth.

And many feel that in all its history, no American, with the possible exception of Abraham Lincoln, has been wiser or greater, or done more for his country, than Benjamin Franklin.

A Hundred Years Later

Postscript

W ORK on electricity continued after Franklin's time, of course. Through the 1800's, great discoveries were made. Chemical batteries were invented that produced a constant flow of electricity. Generators were developed that produced electricity by having steam engines turn wheels between the ends of magnets.

Words were sent across oceans and continents by means of an electric current, as the telegraph and telephone were invented. Electric lights illuminated the nation, and electric motors ran all kinds of gadgets.

In the end, the force of rubbed amber, which had seemed to be of no use for so many centuries, came into its own.

Yet all through the 1800's, no one had any more idea of what the electrical fluid might be than Stephen Gray had had.

Franklin, with his usual uncanny ability to be

ahead of his time, had wondered, once, whether the electrical fluid might not be made up of very tiny particles.

He proved to be correct. Through the 1800's, scientists had come to realize that everything was made up of tiny particles called *atoms*. Electricity went beyond even that, however. In the 1890's, a full century after Franklin's death, scientists discovered that electric current was made up of particles that were far tinier than atoms. These particles were called *electrons*.

In fact, it turned out that the atoms themselves were made up of electrons and other such particles. Each atom contains at least one of each of two different kinds of particles. The electron is one of them and the other is the *proton*. Both the electron and the proton carry an electric charge. The charge on one is exactly equal to the charge on the other, but the two charges are opposite in nature.

Du Fay was right, in a way, after all. There are two different kinds of electrical fluid. The protons contained what Du Fay called "vitreous electricity." The electrons contained his "resinous electricity." To use Franklin's words, the protons were "positive electricity," and the electrons were "negative electricity."

However, Franklin's one-fluid theory was correct, in a way, also. Although there are two differ-

ent electrical fluids, only one of them moves under ordinary conditions.

The protons are very heavy particles that stay in place. The electrons are much lighter (an electron is only $\frac{1}{1836}$ as heavy as a proton), and move easily from one body to another.

Every object is full of electricity, as Franklin had thought. Usually, however, the positive and negative electricity is present in equal quantities, so that there is no sign of electrification. The two types balance each other.

Rubbing glass with silk causes electrons to transfer from one to the other. One object then has more electrons than it should, and the other less. The same is true whenever an object is electrified by rubbing.

Franklin had made only one mistake. He had guessed that the electrical fluid passed from the silk to the glass. That is why he said the glass had a positive or "plus" charge. He had guessed that electrical fluid had been added to it.

He knew he was guessing and that perhaps the fluid moved in the other direction. But he had no way of telling which was the correct direction, and he had a fifty-fifty chance of being right if he just guessed.

But, alas, he was wrong. The electrical fluid (the electrons, that is) passed from the glass to the silk.

The glass had less fluid than it ordinarily had, not more.

A modern electrician always considers electricity to be flowing from the positive side of the circuit to the negative side. That was Franklin's guess. The scientist, however, knows that the current is flowing from the negative side to the positive.

In practical electric work, fortunately, it doesn't really matter which way you consider the current to be flowing, as long as you stick to whatever you decide. It's only when you switch directions in the middle that you have trouble.

It is like people seated at dinner about a round table. Etiquette says that the salad bowl should be to the left of each person. Usually, therefore, each person helps himself from the bowl to his left. If, however, each person were to decide to take the bowl to his right, that would cause no trouble either, as long as *everyone* decided to do it. It is only when some take from the left and some from the right, that there is trouble.

Nor can anyone really blame Franklin for his mistake. It seems to me that any person ought to be allowed one wrong guess in eighty-five years, and Franklin scarcely seems to have made any other wrong ones.

Just one last word, now. What is the negative electric charge present on the electron? What is the

positive electric charge present on the proton? In short, what is electricity?

You know, 2500 years have passed since Thales first began wondering about the answer to that question — and scientists still don't know.